A *Glimpse* OF
HEAVEN

A *Glimpse* OF
HEAVEN

One Woman's Life-Altering Visit with God

JoAnna Oblander

SWEETWATER BOOKS
AN IMPRINT OF CEDAR FORT, INC.
SPRINGVILLE, UTAH

ISBN 13: 978-1-59955-976-6

Published by Sweetwater Books, an imprint of Cedar Fort, Inc.
2373 W. 700 S., Springville, UT 84663
Distributed by Cedar Fort, Inc., www.cedarfort.com

LIBRARY OF CONGRESS CATALOGING-IN-PUBLICATION DATA

Oblander, JoAnna Weekes, 1959- , author.
  A glimpse of heaven : one woman's life-altering visit with God / JoAnna
Weekes Oblander.
    p. cm.
  ISBN 978-1-59955-976-6
  1. Oblander, JoAnna Weekes, 1959- 2. Revelation--Church of Jesus Christ
of Latter-day Saints. 3. Adoption--Religious aspects--Church of Jesus
Christ of Latter-day Saints. 4. Mormon women--Biography. I. Title.

  BX8695.O26A3 2011
  289.3092--dc23
  [B]

2011036945

Cover design by Rebecca Jensen
Cover design © 2012 by Lyle Mortimer
Edited and typeset by Kelley Konzak

Printed in the United States of America

10 9 8 7 6 5 4 3 2 1

Printed on acid-free paper

To Greg, our children, and our family that continues to grow:
You are my greatest blessing.

To adoptive and foster parents who open their hearts and their homes:
God knows your efforts, and this world is a better place because of you.

To adoptive and foster children:
It is in your power, with God's help, to create a loving and meaningful life no matter where you started.

To those who are suffering from depression and ill health:
Life is worth the fight, and caring hearts can be found.

To all who practice the healing arts by allowing their hearts to guide them rather than their pocketbooks:
Your life will be richly blessed in the long term for what you give up in the short term.

To all who strive to make this world a better, more positive place to be:

Thank You.

PRAISE FOR
A *Glimpse* OF HEAVEN

"This glimpse of the preexistence is a helpful guide in maneuvering through life's challenges. The instruction given in this book on how to recognize and follow the spirit is essential information for all. Truly a life-changing experience."

—John and Laurie Raymond

"*A Glimpse of Heaven* offers a powerful case of how spirituality can better our lives. Some people may have their diet and exercise in check—but unless you have a whole integrative approach to life with that crucial connection to spirit, source, God—or whomever God is for you—life just doesn't work."

—Pamela McDonald, NP, author of *The APO E Gene Diet*

"I was looking for something in my life. I didn't know what it was, but I felt that I would recognize it when I found it. I believed there had to be more knowledge, more I could know about my existence and purpose and how to be the real me I was designed to be. I was searching for answers and didn't know where to find them. Within the first few pages of *A Glimpse of Heaven*, I knew that I had found what I had been seeking—this book is filled with answers and was exactly what I had been looking for!"

—Jessica Oliver

"Grabbing you at the first page, this book is much more than a story about finding an adoptive son in a foreign country or healing from depression and migraine headaches.

"It is a personal odyssey of one woman's failures and triumphs as she learns to communicate with Heavenly Beings. With much effort and obedience on her part, she learns how to listen and identify voices of truth which come in many different ways. . . .

"Some may not understand this book, but even the skeptics will admit that it contains much food for thought and will prompt us to examine the Lord's hand in our lives. I recommend it."

—Lauris Butler Hunter, Gaithersburg, Maryland

chapter one

TAKEN BACK TO HEAVENLY FATHER

*A*T day's end I sat on my bed overcome with convulsive tears. My will to live had been obliterated. Mental imbalance caused by severe depression and a handful of negative encounters with less-than-empathetic bill collectors had been the final victors on that summer day in 2002. Holding onto life had proven itself too hard.

Throughout those dark months of depression, necessity had dictated that life be handled in small increments. Holding on for twenty-four hours was often too difficult. Holding on for another breath, another minute, maybe even another hour was the only realistic goal. It was the only way I had been able to keep my suicidal desires at bay.

Inside my once joyous and vibrant soul brewed an emotional storm. My mind screamed I didn't want to live, but my heart passionately insisted that life needed to be clung to. My battle was lonely and intense despite having loving supporters around me. Each day seemed like a grueling marathon as I worked to get my health and former happiness back.

By the end of my traumatic day, wanting an end to the pain, my heart admitted defeat. My emotional avalanche had battered me so severely that I was unwilling to consider giving life another chance. Every depressive trigger that was associated with my depression had been pulled, every ounce of my resolve had vanished, and I was done.

The only thing that had given me a will to live was my love for my husband and children and their love for me. As I sat on my bed crying, no doubt remained in my depressed mind that my family would be better off without me burdening their lives.

God has always been a crucial part of my life. Somehow, even in the depths of my gloomy battle, I knew that my Creator had worked hard to help me. Not wanting to exclude Him from the decision I had made, I crept out of bed to say my prayers one last time.

I didn't make any requests for help that night. I was certain that I was beyond help. I calmly explained to God that He knew and I knew that I had given my fight everything I had. I told God that I was done and that I had nothing more to give. I apologized for not being able to do better. I thanked Him for the good things that He had blessed me with. Then, I told Him that I could not endure the pain any longer and that if He chose to send me to hell that would be okay—I knew with certainty that hell could not be worse than what I was currently suffering. I explained that I would be ending my life the following day and from there what happened to me would be in His hands. I then crawled back into bed and cried myself to sleep.

I had been asleep for just a short time when an angel appeared above me, stretched forth his arms, and beckoned me to come with him. He reached for my hand and pulled my spirit toward him. The separation from my body occurred effortlessly. As the angel pulled my spirit out of my body, he pulled me through the west wall of my bedroom toward the stars in the southwest sky. We traveled through a large conduit. I could see the outline of the conduit, though the walls were clear. My angel was insistent that we hurry. Not saying a word, he communicated that he had something important to show me. Never letting go of my hand, he stayed just in front of me until we reached our destination. Though we moved rapidly, there were no familiar sensations of travel. In a short amount of time, we approached a large complex of rooms.

As we approached, I recognized the complex. I knew I had been there many times before. The complex was filled with classrooms, students, and instructors. As I looked at each of the classrooms, the walls melted away so that I could see inside each classroom and into the hallways, as I desired.

Gazing at the rooms, I realized that I had returned to the sphere of existence that I had been a part of before I was born. I was familiar with everything there. I knew the layout of the complex. I knew what subjects were being taught in certain classrooms. I recognized many of the instructors.

I never saw the outside walls of the complex, only the hallways and classrooms within. The classrooms were large, like college class-rooms, but without the theater-style seating college classrooms so often have. There were dozens of classrooms in the complex, con-nected by an orderly system of hallways—all on one level, which spread out over an area that would encompass several city blocks. Each classroom had a specific topic being covered, but the topics were not typical high school or college fare. Instead, the topics being cov-ered related to the types of experiences it would be possible to have on earth. Each classroom I observed had one to three instructors at the front of the room actively providing information on their topic and answering questions from their students. Numbers in each class seemed to vary between about twenty-five and sixty students. The students I saw were not children but adults, and they sat in desks that were lined up in rows just like a typical high school classroom. The classrooms seemed to be equipped with podiums, projector screens, chalkboards, and other typical furnishings of school classrooms, but my attention was never on those items—my attention was always focused on the conversations taking place in those classrooms.

The students were being taught what it would be like on earth. Everyone at the complex was looking forward to his or her experi-ence on earth. All were eagerly learning and making decisions. Each of us was learning about and making decisions in regard to the type of experiences that we would have on earth. Nobody was worried about whether they would be rich or famous, beautiful or handsome, tall or short. We did not even worry about whether we would be healthy or well. Instead, decisions were being made based on which experiences would help us become perfect like Heavenly Father. Great concern was given to furthering talents, improving strengths, obtaining greater intelligence, and refining our ability to love.

The sole purpose of this complex was to prepare God's children to come to earth. Earth was the next training ground. On earth, we would learn to use and exercise faith. Learning to use faith was an important step in becoming like our Heavenly Father, and we all took it very seriously. Vital instruction was being given, and important decisions were being made. Everyone was eager to learn to live by faith and prove himself or herself on earth. That was the ultimate goal there; we were all passionate about becoming like our Heavenly Father.

My attention was easily diverted as I watched students and instructors exchange questions and replies. Eventually, my angel had to turn my attention away from the classrooms. He directed my attention to a meeting room to the left of the classrooms that I had been watching.

As I looked at the room, I could see that Heavenly Father was in the room. I easily recognized Him, even from a distance. He was approaching the door that accessed the hallway. I could tell that He was able to see through the walls just as I was, and we both could see that two individuals were approaching the door from the hallway. I was surprised to see that I recognized the two individuals. It was me and the man who is now my husband Greg. Somehow, as I watched, I knew that Greg and I had been summoned to a special meeting with Heavenly Father.

As I saw myself and Greg approach the door, the blocks on my memory were removed. Everything I knew and everything that I had ever experienced in that prebirth existence was restored. My memories were not just of a short lifetime or existence; they stretched through eons of time. Much that I remembered was relevant to Greg as well. I was able to remember all of the experiences that we had shared. I knew when we were scheduled to be born and I knew that it had been planned that Greg and I would be together on earth. I was allowed to completely comprehend who I was and what I had accomplished in that realm of my existence.

My surprise in seeing myself approach the room paled in comparison to the surprise I felt when I was allowed to recall who I was—who I really was. I was taken aback by the immensity and the vastness of the experiences that I'd had.

I have always believed that my spirit existed prior to being born on earth. Other life experiences had confirmed this belief. However, nothing I had believed even remotely prepared me for what I found in this celestial realm.

As a child, I was taught that when we are born, a veil is placed over our minds, which keeps us from remembering our premortal life. I had envisioned a sort of semitransparent veil—a veil that would occasionally let fragments of memory slip through. Here, with the veil removed from my mind, I realized that the veil that is placed over our memories of our premortal lives is more like a wall of armored steel. Once the blocks were removed from my memory, I was a completely different person. Gone were my insecurities and doubts. (Gone was my depression.) Eternal truth and God's love dominated that realm. As a result, my confidence was supreme. I struggle to find words that even begin to describe what it felt like to be me in that sphere of existence. My entire being was infused with love and gratitude and devotion to God. My existence there was devoted to furthering Heavenly Father's work. My intelligence was absolutely incredible. The atmosphere was glorious and radiated love. My feelings and understanding were not bound by the same earthly restrictions that we have as mortals. It was magnificent beyond description.

It was so wonderful to have my full eternal perspective back. It was completely exhilarating. Being allowed to know my strengths and abilities again was the most wonderful reunion I have ever experienced, and the reunion was with the *real* me. In place of my mortal doubts and fears was a powerful and peaceful assurance of the immensity of my capabilities. I was completely amazed at the breadth and depth of my abilities, talents, and intelligence in the premortal realm. I was truly amazing and yet I did not stand out from the crowd—we were all amazing. My premortal self was inspirational beyond description. However, there, rather than viewing my abilities with any degree of arrogance, I viewed each of my gifts, talents, and abilities as immense blessings that allowed me to serve Heavenly Father with greater purpose and strength. That was what mattered to me—that was what mattered to each of us who were at the training complex. There, in my premortal state, my motivations and desires were pure. I loved Heavenly Father so intensely. I completely desired to serve Him and do His work.

I knew that although preparations were being made for the next stage of our eternal progression, such had not always been the case.

Some great battles had taken place in that heavenly sphere. Those who were in this complex were some of the victors in that Great War. However, those battles had not been battles of physical force. They had been battles of truth and intelligence. Those who sided with and had fought for Heavenly Father had passed a great and vital test and now, as a result, were receiving instruction in the classrooms in preparation for their next sphere of existence. Each one who had sided with our Heavenly Father in the Great War would experience mortality on earth.

In that sphere of existence, we were constantly surrounded by a spirit of truth and intelligence and love. It completely emanated through us and around us. As I viewed everything around me from a mortal perspective, I realized that it was our removal from that environment that made mortality so difficult.

I became so caught up in my experience of being reunited with my memories that, a second time, the angel had to redirect my attention. He insisted that I watch as Heavenly Father ushered Greg and me into the room.

I turned my attention toward the events that were taking place in the room that Heavenly Father was in.

As Greg and I entered the room, Heavenly Father grasped our hands, and then he tenderly hugged each of us for a few moments. As Heavenly Father ushered us into the room, he motioned toward two high-backed chairs. The room we were in was not used for classroom instruction but was utilized for personal meetings with Heavenly Father. It was a large, square room—about forty feet by forty feet—but it was not as large as the classrooms with students that I had observed. The room, including the walls, was completely vacant except for the two high-backed chairs, which were positioned close to each other in the middle of the room—not directly across from each other but angled so that those sitting in the chairs were close enough to easily converse with one another.

As I watched Greg and I enter the room, I could both observe the scene beside my angel and feel the experience again as though it were happening to me for the first time. Looking upon the scene as I stood beside my angel, I knew I was being allowed to see a meeting that had already occurred.

My angel and I observed the meeting just outside one of the corners of the room. However, because we could see through walls as though they did not exist, the walls in no way impeded my ability to see and hear every detail of the meeting. I was able to be an unseen observer of the meeting as though it were taking place in real time.

Though I was able to watch and listen from outside the room, most of my memories are of the feelings and thoughts that I had as I reexperienced the meeting, sitting in the chair close to Heavenly Father.

As I watched the meeting commence from outside the room, it was like watching a movie in which I was playing the lead role. I saw Heavenly Father instruct me to sit in the chair on the left as he sat in the chair on the right. Greg stood behind my chair. As I sat down in the chair, my point of view as an outside observer changed. Once I was seated in the chair, I experienced the remainder of the meeting as an active participant. I somehow knew that Heavenly Father had already discussed with Greg His intent for this meeting. And, although I strongly sensed that Greg was there to be a support for me, I knew that he had also been a part of the decision-making process that had brought us to this meeting. As Greg stood behind me, he massaged my shoulders with his hands as if to reassure me. I was grateful for his comforting touch. I readily caught on to Greg's cue—I knew that I was going to be required to make an important decision.

Our spirits operated much like our mortal bodies in that realm; though I cannot remember smelling or tasting anything, I feel certain those senses did exist there and my ability to touch, see, and communicate manifested themselves just like I am accustomed to in this life. Though we spoke to each other using words, I cannot say for sure whether we had to speak with our mouths to actually communicate those words. Either way, our ability to interact with each other seemed perfectly normal.

Greg is now my husband, but in this prebirth sphere, we were not married. Previous to my return to this premortal sphere, Greg and I had often expressed feelings that heavenly forces had guided our relationship. It seemed to both of us that our coming together had not been mere coincidence but rather a carefully orchestrated course of events that had been put in place by heavenly forces. From the time that we had first started dating, it had felt more like we were old friends being reunited rather than two people dating each other for the first time. For years, Greg had joked that he had loved me forever. Heaven seemed to whisper to our hearts things that we could not confirm but sensed nonetheless. As I watched the meeting begin, I realized that those whisperings had communicated things to me that my spirit *knew* but my mind was not allowed to remember.

I experienced the entire meeting as it had occurred the first time, with the same thoughts, the same emotions, and the same responses, with one exception: as I initially looked into God's face, I had a brief mortal thought. As I looked at Him, I was amazed at how familiar I was with His face, His features, and His expressions. I was astounded that I could have forgotten a face that was so easily recognizable to me and that I knew so well. This testified to me of how powerful the block on my memory had been. I knew that only a powerful block could keep me from remembering this Being whom I knew so well, loved so much, and had been so devoted to.

His face was warm and smiling and full of love. It was totally radiant. His Being was totally pure and totally perfect. While I can no longer remember His features, I do remember that His face was perfect. However, it was not His features that made His face perfect; it was His spirit, which emanated through His features. I have never seen a more perfect face. I could have gazed at His face indefinitely.

Heavenly Father's love was totally enveloping. It was like having a warm blanket fresh out of the dryer wrapped around you, but one that not only gives warmth to your skin but whose warmth also penetrates to your core. I basked in His love for me. It was so uplifting and inspiring.

I remember being amazed that so many of us are so careless in our relationship with Him in this mortal sphere. I was also amazed that so many of us in mortality place such limitations on His abilities. If my abilities in the premortal sphere were commanding, His were all encompassing. I was a work in the making; He is a completed work. My intelligence was great and growing; His intelligence is without a single gap.

It was now time for our special meeting to begin. Heavenly

Father initiated our meeting by explaining His purpose for our intimate gathering. He gently clasped my hands in His. He told me that he had an important assignment for me. He explained what the assignment was and that it would be very difficult. Then He showed me how my life on earth would proceed if I chose to accept my assignment. This He did by motioning for me to look through the conduit that my angel had brought me through. At the bottom of the conduit I could see earth and every detail of my life as it would transpire. It was as though we could use Google Earth to zoom in on my life. We were able to look through the conduit as though the distance between the room we were in and earth was only fifteen to twenty feet (rather than stretching through vast galaxies). We zoomed in on all the events of my life, seeing all the individuals and locations that would be involved in my life experiences. Within minutes, we were able to fast forward through my life from the beginning to the end. Yet, even though the amount of time it took to preview my life was quick, my comprehension of all that I was shown was complete. However, I knew that the scenarios that I saw concerning my earth life were those that would occur if I stayed close to Heavenly Father and made good choices. I likewise knew that any errors in decision-making that I made on earth would or could change the landscape of my life as I was seeing it.

I saw those on earth who I would interact with. I saw what my life would be like both as a child and as an adult. I saw happy moments, great difficulties, and everything in between. Within moments, I was shown everything.

When He was finished showing me my earthly life, He told me that He would understand if I chose not to accept the assignment. He told me that He knew that the assignment that He was asking me to accept would be very difficult and challenging. He also told me of His confidence in me and that if I utilized His help, I would succeed.

I knew the choice was truly mine. I was being asked to make a choice, but there was no undue pressure. The only pressure that presented itself in any way was my desire to serve my Creator with devotion and perfection. I was keenly aware that my Father in Heaven would never rob me of my ability to choose.

I knew that several aspects of the assignment that I was being asked to accept were necessary in order for some greater purposes to be accomplished.

After He finished telling me about and showing me my assignment, Heavenly Father told me that there would always be evidences of Him to remind me that He was there. He told me that there would be times that I would not be able to feel Him with me, but if I would always stay close to Him, I would make it through all of the difficulties and would be able to accomplish all that I was being asked to undertake. He reminded me again that He would never, ever, even for the briefest moment, leave me. He then reminded me that Greg would be there to help me as well.

I'm not sure how to describe the emotions that coursed through me as I considered whether or not to accept the assignment. I don't think that what I felt could be described as fear, but I know that the immensity of the assignment weighed on me greatly. I had not been comforted by what I had been shown of my life on earth. Never before in my premortal life had I ever felt so overwhelmed. I briefly considered not taking the assignment. I speculated that it would be better to let someone else take the assignment rather than risk the possibility of failing Heavenly Father.

Aware of the thoughts I was having, Heavenly Father reminded me again that, as long as I remembered Him and stayed close to Him, I would not fail. He again acknowledged that my assignment would be difficult but then lovingly stressed that if I followed His guidance and remembered Him, I would ultimately succeed. He also reminded me that although the forces of evil were strong, His power was supreme and would ultimately overcome all evil.

I knew that Heavenly Father could not lie. I realized that He would not ask me to accept anything that I could not accomplish if I used His help. I knew of His great desire to see me and each of His children succeed. Therefore, I knew He would never ask me to accept any assignment in which there were any doubts or reservations about my ability to accomplish the task. As those thoughts came to my mind, I chose to accept Heavenly Father's assignment for me. As I did so, He gently squeezed my hands and verbally acknowledged the correctness of my decision. And then, as though He were trying to make sure that I never forgot, He once again reminded me that I would always need to *remember* Him and that He would always be with me. The word *remember* now seems as if it has been imprinted into the cement of my mind.

Heavenly Father then looked up at Greg and nodded to him that our meeting was finished. We stood up, and Heavenly Father took me into His arms and embraced me for several moments. His embrace was warm and loving. I was not able to differentiate between His resurrected body and my body, which was still only spirit matter (not yet combined with mortal matter). As He held me in His arms, I felt His love and comfort infuse into my being. He told me of His love for me and thanked me for my willingness to serve Him. He thanked Greg for being there with us and for His willingness to help me carry out my assignment.

I was so full of gratitude during our last moments in the room together. I was grateful for Heavenly Father's love and perfection and for His confidence in me. Though I felt some apprehension about the enormity of the assignment I had just accepted, I felt peace knowing that Greg would be with me and that I would be completely and perfectly supported by the perfect Being who was the Father of my spirit.

As Greg and I moved toward the door to leave the room, my point of view changed again, and my angel took me back to my body, still lying on the bed in my bedroom, through the same conduit that we traveled through before.

As soon as I was returned to my body, I awakened. I was not aware of my trip back to earth, and I felt no transition as my spirit reentered my body. However, some of the wonderful feelings and emotions that I had just been a part of accompanied me back to my body. As I was reunited with my body, I again felt the sensations of pain that were such a pervasive part of my life during that time period and that had been absent in the premortal realm. I felt extremely blessed because of the significantly expanded understanding that I was now blessed with, but it was difficult to be reunited with the intense pain once again. I felt so grateful for my experience, yet it was very difficult to know that in addition to my pain resuming, I would not be able to retain all of the knowledge and feelings that I had just been a part of. Although I could vividly remember the major details of the experience that I had just had, the powerful veil on my memory was immediately back in place. I could no longer remember the details of Heavenly Father's face or most of the details of the assignment that I had accepted. The details of my life as I had been allowed to see them through the conduit vanished from my memory as well.

I immediately knew that I had been allowed to revisit those moments in my premortal life in order to gain the strength and understanding I would need to keep hanging on through my severe depression. I remained awake the rest of the night—what little was left of it. I reflected over and over again on the experience that I had just been granted. Though I received very little sleep that night and felt physically tired, I felt so overwhelmed emotionally and mentally that sleep was impossible. It was approximately 4:00 in the morning when I returned to my body, and all I could do was lie in bed trying to absorb what had just happened.

chapter Two

LIFE IS WORTH
THE JOURNEY

The next morning I approached my life on earth with a much deeper appreciation of Heavenly Father and the blessings that were present in my life. My decision to end my life was changed, and my understanding of the purposes of this life and its relevance to the rest of eternity was imprinted with a much deeper spiritual maturity. Although my depression remained as severe as it was before my experience, my dedication to succeeding in the ordeal that I called my life was backed by a much more powerful resolve.

After my return to earth, the preexisting beliefs I had concerning life and death were not changed. In the celestial realm, everything I saw confirmed the correctness of my beliefs. However, my overall perspective was changed dramatically. Death holds no fear for me now; what does frighten me is the possibility that I might in some way fail my Creator or not fully accomplish my assignment. I will never take my relationship with my Heavenly Father for granted or minimize its importance ever again. I have an unshakable respect for life, and I know that it is of the utmost importance that I work toward accomplishing my full potential and the mission that I accepted before I was born.

Initially, I believed that overcoming my depression and my other health problems would be hastened because of my experience in premortality. That was not to be the case, but my experience there empowered me to change my perspective and to be more teachable.

Once upon a time (as though life were a fairy tale), I used to think that life should be fair. I used to be what I call a "counter." A counter keeps track of wrongs and rights and is convinced that the rights should outweigh the wrongs or, at the very least, they should be equal. Not surprisingly, I often found that the wrongs in my life easily outweighed the rights. My perspective was often skewed by my mistaken belief that they should at least equal each other. As a result, I frequently felt resentment in regard to the difficult circumstances that life often seemed to hand me.

However, I have never been inclined to want to give up those lessons learned or the understanding I have gained from those very same experiences that I considered unfair and difficult. That is a contradiction I once had difficulty understanding. I have heard countless others express the same sentiment. We all want life to be a breeze and yet none of us are willing to let go of the wisdom we have gained because life *isn't* a breeze.

Now, despite my memory being veiled once again, I understand why life needs to have challenges. I also understand why we all inherently value knowledge and experience—even when gaining them involves suffering and pain.

We haven't come to earth so that we can enjoy a vacation. Our spirits, that part of us that we are the most familiar with, are on a quest. Although we cannot remember that realm from which we have come, we still bring with us stardust that ties us to our Creator and to the existence we knew there. Our spirits inherently know we need growth—that is what we came here for.

Those experiences that require us to stretch and to grow and to overcome are our very best teachers. As I watched those classrooms in the premortal realm, no one was looking to make life easy. Everyone was looking for those experiences that would give him or her maximum growth. It didn't matter whether our lives would be cut short or whether we lived to a ripe old age, whether we were ugly or beautiful, whether we were rich or poor. What did matter was how we handled our lives once we were here. It mattered that we develop honorable and praiseworthy attributes and did not succumb to selfishness, greed, or malice. Goodness was to be sought. Evil was to be shunned.

We all knew that there would be adversity here. We also knew that Heavenly Father is perfect and could not lie to us. So, when we were taught in premortality that it was possible to learn to live by faith with that veil over our memories of our premortal experience and to become like Father in Heaven, we not only believed Him, we were eager to be given the chance.

chapter Three

A VISIT FROM HEAVEN

24 Years Earlier (1978)

Greg and I had been married for less than three months. As newlyweds, we were feeling euphoric about life with each other and serious thoughts about starting a family had not yet materialized. We were young and not in a big hurry, and it seemed as though we had plenty of time to get that all figured out. We knew that because of some of the female reproductive issues that I had, starting a family was probably not going to be an easy accomplishment. So, for the time being, we were feeling content to just enjoy each other and our new life together.

One night, toward the end of our first three months of marriage, Greg and I were preparing for bed. During that time, I had been experiencing a lot of lower back pain, so I normally lay in bed during our nightly prayers together. That night, Greg felt strongly impressed that we both needed to be on our knees for prayers. I got out of bed on the right side, and Greg moved over next to me. As we knelt beside each other and we began to say our prayer, a miracle began to unfold. Heaven opened up to us.

We both saw five spirits in our bedroom. There were four spirits standing close to each other to our right near the foot of our bed. The fifth spirit, a male, stood just inside our bedroom doorway behind and to the left of the other four spirits. Each of the spirits was an adult and appeared to be approximately twenty-five to thirty years of age. My husband saw each of the spirits enter the bedroom. I did not

17

see them until they reached the end of our bed.

When I say that we saw the spirits in our bedroom, I mean that we did see them, but neither of us opened our eyes. I don't remember the words of our prayer that night, but I remember what I saw through my closed eyes and how I felt as I saw our heavenly visitors. Each of them was clothed in white robes and had a radiance that was glorious. I could see and feel their immense purity, spiritual strength, and love.

I have always believed that it takes a spirit combined with a physical body to comprise a living soul. Realizing that spirits are immortal and don't age like mortal bodies, I thought I could be seeing deceased grandparents. To me, it initially seemed like the four spirits who stood near our bed were couples. I sensed that they knew each other and each "couple" seemed especially close. The females stood on each end of the foursome. The males stood by each other in the middle of the spirits. No words were communicated during their visitation.

The moment we opened our eyes at the conclusion of our prayer, the spirits were gone. The spiritual atmosphere in the room was very strong. Somewhat in shock and while still on our knees, we turned toward each other, not knowing what to say. We each were wondering if the other had seen what had just taken place in our bedroom. I tentatively asked Greg, "Did you just see . . . ? He responded, "Yeah . . . did you see . . . ?" I quietly said, "I just saw four spirits standing next to each other at the end of our bed with another spirit behind them by the bedroom door." Greg replied, "Yes, I saw them too." With the spirit of reverence that we both were feeling, we climbed into bed and sat in bed for several minutes awestruck by what had just happened. Because of my initial impressions that each "couple" had a special bond with each other, I asked, "Do you think maybe they were some of our grandparents that we never knew?" "No," Greg replied, "They were our children." The moment he told me that the spirits were our unborn children, warmth filled my heart and I too knew that the four spirits who had stood at the foot of our bed were our children. Once I knew who the spirits were, I instantly knew that our children had stood in the order that they would be born. Greg knew that as well. We knew that the first to be born would be the female spirit that stood to our left (and who Greg had seen enter first) and that the female spirit who stood on the far right (who Greg saw enter last) would be the last born. Then, we both began to contemplate who the fifth spirit was. Shaking his head and shrugging his shoulders, Greg made the comment, "I don't know who the fifth spirit was, but maybe our children needed an escort to come here tonight." I asked, "Do you think he really was their escort?" He shook his head again and replied, "Maybe. I don't know." Neither of us understood the purpose of the visit from our unborn children and neither of us knew who the male spirit was who had stood in our bedroom doorway. We could only guess that maybe unborn spirits had to have a special escort to come to earth, but for us, that was all it was—a guess.

chapter four

BECOMING A FAMILY

Over the next few weeks, we pondered our miraculous experience. We were clueless as to why we had been allowed to see our unborn children. However, just like everything Heavenly Father orchestrates, the timing of the visit by our unborn children quickly made sense.

In regard to babies and pregnancy, I was the clueless type. I knew virtually nothing about the well-known experiences that commonly accompany both being pregnant and life with a baby.

It was mid-September, and I had determined I was having a mild yet miserably prolonged case of the flu. Though I was feeling nauseated and drained of energy, I was not vomiting or suffering from other flu-like symptoms such as body aches, so I thought I was just having a hard time kicking the tail end of the flu. One Sunday, I felt a little bit better, so I went to church. A friend commented on how tired I looked. I told her that I had felt nauseated for two or three weeks and that I couldn't understand why my flu symptoms seemed so determined to hang on.

She looked at me, smiled, and said, "It sounds like you're pregnant!" I was incredulous even though, just weeks before, my husband and I had had the bedtime visit from our unborn children. From that special visit, I knew that I was going to eventually give birth to four children, but I was astounded to think that the journey to motherhood may have already begun.

The results of a pregnancy test quickly confirmed that it had indeed commenced. Morning sickness and lack of energy brought their unique challenges, as did the knowledge that I was going to be a mother and that my first daughter was on her way. I felt like such a spiritual newbie. I had always been spiritually inclined, but everything I had seen of our children in their spirit form told me that I was going to give birth to spiritual giants. How does someone like me give adequate mothering and be an example to a spiritual giant? It was a question that haunted me.

As knowledge of my pregnancy spread, I would often get questions about whether I thought I was going to have a girl or a boy. I would answer that I thought I was going to have a girl. Ultrasounds were in use by then, but the images were not terribly clear, and I never felt inclined to have one because I already knew what I was having. For me, that was never a doubt. However, when people would then ask why I thought I was having a girl, I would have to do a little backpedaling. I didn't feel that it was appropriate to share our experience of seeing our children as spirits. So I would usually just say that I somehow felt very strongly that I was going to have a girl.

Our first daughter, Melissa, arrived in May of 1979. She was sweet and precious, and the love and concern that I felt for her as she grew within me for nine months only grew stronger after her birth.

Like most new parents, we were in awe of this cherished bundle who was our firstborn. However, my awe did not eliminate my naïveté regarding babies. The first night that we brought Melissa home, I laid her in her bassinet when she fell asleep around our usual bedtime, and we went to bed as well. About four in the morning, Greg was trying to wake me up (which I thought was so rude). "Jo, wake up . . . Jo, wake up . . . Jo, wake up—the baby!" To which I replied, "I don't hear the baby." Greg said, "That's my point. We should have heard her by now—we need to make sure she is okay." Not knowing that babies wake up during the night, I thought Greg was being highly overzealous in his concern about our baby. Therefore, I told him, "You go check her." I wasn't feeling inclined to be awake, and given my lack of knowledge in the whole baby business, I was definitely not feeling the concern that he was. Greg then got out of bed and listened closely to the baby for several minutes, making sure she was still breathing. She was breathing just fine and she was sleeping peacefully, so I thought it was time for Greg to quit worrying and let both of us get some rest. He continued to worry the rest of those early morning hours, and I went back to sleep and slept like a log.

It probably didn't help my motherly cluelessness that Melissa was the miracle baby that everyone dreams of having but that odds say will never happen. Not only did she sleep through the night that very first night that we brought her home, but she slept through the night every night after that too! Personally, I like to think that it was Heavenly Father's recognition of how badly I need my sleep. (I know that those that have spent sleepless nights with babies for all the various reasons that there are will disagree!) In all reality, I have no clue as to why we were blessed with a baby that slept through the night, but I am very grateful!

Despite all my cluelessness about babies, I loved being a new mother. I babysat as a teen, and though I had enjoyed taking care of babies, motherhood added a joyous dimension to my life that I had never anticipated. I worked full time up until Melissa's birth, but Greg and I decided that I needed to be a stay-at-home mother, so I did not return to work after my maternity leave ended. I loved my new job of being a full-time mother. I loved holding our baby daughter and talking to her and sharing all her firsts with Greg.

Melissa seemed determined to come to earth and get the essential steps of baby advancement behind her. She was always a wonderful sleeper, but once the initial few months were behind us, her waking hours were filled with her earnest efforts to learn how to roll over, crawl, walk, and so on. At nine months, she was both walking and talking, and she was a handful to keep up with. At fifteen months, she had a vocabulary of over 115 words.

Right around Melissa's first birthday, I began to feel incessant nausea once again. Our first son was on his way. I never questioned the gender of our children as I carried each one—I always knew what they were going to be. Instead, I would wonder what they were going to be like and what they would look like and how I would be able to do justice to the responsibility that was mine to raise them.

Seeing our children prior to their births predisposed me to think of them as beings with immense spiritual propensity. Our first son, Chad, seemed intent on making me recognize that each was his or her own person and that they all had other traits worth noting as well. He seemed particularly intent on letting me know he had a great knack for teasing. The last twenty-one days of carrying Chad were spent in false labor. The first trip to the hospital had the nurses asking me if this was my first baby. The intense contractions I was feeling on the second trip to the hospital abruptly ended just as we arrived at the hospital. Chad finally arrived on our third trip to the hospital in February of 1981.

All of our children love to tease me (a trait that they inherited from their father), but Chad is the one who really loves to get a rise out of me. Chad was the one who stood tallest as we saw the spirits of our children. Now full grown, he is also tallest of our children as adults.

Not to be outdone by his older sister, Chad walked at nine months with barely a week or two of crawling previous to walking. Seeing them as spirits, I had sensed the closeness of the first two spirits (Melissa and Chad) and the last two. As young siblings, Melissa and Chad seemed to completely forget any close relationships they had enjoyed in the premortal existence. Instead, they often drove each other crazy with their differences.

I don't know how old they were when we shared our experience of seeing them prior to their births, but it was never made a secret. So, at times when they were quarreling, I would try to remind them that I knew they loved each other and that they had a close bond with each other. They would both look at me like I had a screw loose.

Chad was just over two years old when I started having incessant nausea and tiredness for the third time. By that time, I was fully immersed in the motherhood experience and I was wondering how I was going to keep up with a third child. (It was always difficult to imagine having any energy when I was in the throes of constant morning sickness.)

By the time she was about four or five years old, Melissa had grown out of the bouncing with energy all day stage and had started to settle down to an energy level that I found more manageable. Chad, however, was high energy coupled with boy genes, and it was all I could do to keep up.

In January 1984, our second son, Ryan, made his entrance into the world. In keeping with Ryan's personality, he made sure he made his entrance in his own unique way. When I labored to deliver his older brother and sister, the moment doctors broke my water, labor picked up in intensity significantly, dilation was complete within a few contractions, and the baby was delivered within fifteen to twenty minutes. So when my water broke on its own with Ryan, all I could think of was my history with his brother and sister, and I was so overwhelmed with the thought of delivering the baby before we got to the hospital that I can safely say I was of no help to Greg at all in getting our two young children up and ready to go. Somehow we (Greg) got the kids to his mom, and we made it to the hospital.

Despite my panic, there was never any real need to hurry because labor didn't set in after my water broke, and Ryan was not in a big hurry to be born. As far as he was concerned, there were still lots of hours left to get the job done. For those not familiar with the birthing process, you may need to know that once a woman's water has broken, hospitals are adamant that a baby be delivered within a short amount of time.

What that meant for me was experiencing even more panic. I had my babies naturally without the help of pain killers such as epidurals. My previous two deliveries had already indoctrinated me that giving birth is not a pain-free endeavor. However, I also knew that if I had to be induced, the pain I was going to have to go through (without pain medication) was going to increase exponentially.

So, at the advice of my midwife, we walked around the hospital to try to get my contractions going. Though there was no change, we continued to walk around the hospital, and we walked a mile each way from the hospital to the courthouse in downtown Billings to see my father-in-law. We walked from about 8:00 a.m. to 4:30 p.m. with no significant contractions setting in. Between 4:30 and 5:00, I was told that my time was up and that they were going to have to induce me. I pleaded for one more chance to try walking to get some productive labor going. I don't know if they saw the panic in my face and had a moment of mercy or if they envisioned having to listen to me scream once I was hooked up to the IV, but they agreed to give me one more chance. Apparently, my last conversation with my midwife finally got Ryan's attention. As I exited through the door of the birthing room to go walk one last time, a contraction so intense that it kept me from moving hit. I sensed that serious labor had finally arrived, and we turned around and went back into the birthing room. I then gave birth to Ryan just over an hour later.

Ryan was a more mellow personality than his older siblings. I didn't have to worry much about him running ahead of me. Instead, I had to worry that something would get his attention and I would unknowingly leave him behind. Ryan was my first child to love a Binky. He loved his Nuk pacifier but insisted that he suck on it upside down. He never talked much but always made grunting sounds with his pacifier in his mouth. His favorite trick was to twirl his pacifier with his tongue. When he finally allowed us to take it from him at the age of 2, to our surprise, we found that not only could he talk, he could talk in complete sentences!

Our entire family likes to joke that Ryan has always insisted on doing things in his own time frame and in his own way. And that is a characteristic about him that we all love and adore.

I was not feeling ready when my fourth and final experience with feeling nauseated 24-7 came. After my previous three bouts of feeling like I had the flu for nine months, I had hoped to have a little more reprieve before I had to go through a full nine months of morning sickness again. I was also concerned about how I was going to keep up with four children. Ryan was now about a year old, and our home had three very active young children. Ryan was not just walking, he was running, and he had discovered that virtually anything can be climbed. Chad added his own brand of excitement as his mischievous curiosity led him to lock himself in an old refrigerator, attempt to plug keys into an electrical socket, see how far he could push his older sister before she started screaming, and other antics that frequently horrified his mother. Melissa was five going on twenty-five, and she was pretty sure that her mother was failing miserably with her younger brothers. And many days, I did not feel I could disagree.

With three children exhibiting such unique and strong personalities, I often worried that our fourth child would get lost in the shuffle. I wondered how she would be able to make her own mark in our family with such a strong-willed group of siblings to contend with.

Nicole arrived in November of 1985 during a severe winter cold snap. Billings, Montana, was blanketed in snow and experiencing subzero temperatures the day that Nicole arrived. Nicole was due about two weeks before Thanksgiving, but I carried each of my children about two weeks past the due date that I was given. As Thanksgiving approached, I started praying hard that I would not have to miss Thanksgiving dinner with our family. My prayers were granted. I enjoyed a wonderful Thanksgiving dinner and day with our family.

We had prearranged for Greg's dad and stepmom to help with our children when I went into labor. They had family members from out of town staying with them for the holiday, so when I started feeling some stronger contractions around 10:00 p.m. on Thanksgiving Day, we decided to call for them to come and stay with our kids while I went and got checked, reasoning it was better to disturb them at 10:30 p.m. rather than at 2:00 or 3:00 a.m. My contractions were not terribly strong, and I thought I was being a bit overzealous about going to the hospital so soon, but I didn't want to disrupt their sleep in the middle of the night. We got to the hospital about 11:30, and when they checked me about ten minutes later, I was dilated to a six. Surprising everyone involved in the process (including me), Nicole was born just after midnight the day after Thanksgiving.

The next day, as I held Nicole in my arms, I cried. I knew that she was going to be my last baby. Although enduring nine months of morning sickness was never fun, I loved watching each of my babies grow and progress, watching their personalities blossom, and holding and playing with them.

As it turned out, my concern about Nicole being lost in the shuffle was completely unfounded. In fact, my family now regularly teases and chastises me for those past prayers and concerns. They will turn to me and say, "Why did you have to pray that she would not be lost in the shuffle?," a comment that is always made in reference to the fact that Nicole is one of the most outgoing members of our family. As an adult, Nicole has gained greater confidence in her family's ability to function without her assistance. However, as a child, she seemed to be quite certain that she needed to whip the rest of us into shape. It was as though she was amazed that any of us had survived or functioned at any reasonable level prior to her arrival in our family!

As noted earlier, Nicole and Ryan have remained true to the closeness that I perceived was present with each "couple" when we saw them as spirits. They are very close and have been close since they were very young. It has been heartwarming for me to see all four of our children have close relationships with each other as they have advanced into adulthood.

When I began my journey into motherhood with all of the pre-conceived notions that I had as a result of seeing our children as spirits, I was intimidated to know all that I lacked as a mother. As my children grew, I consistently felt too inexperienced and too inca-pable of being the mother they deserved. Now that they are adults, I look back over my experience of raising them, and I am not as hard on myself as I once was. I see the people that my children are, and I smile, my heart overflowing with pride. My children are good people. They are responsible, hardworking, family-oriented, and loving individuals.

Yet, for all their goodness and abilities, my children do not yet grasp their innate gifts and strengths as my husband and I witnessed them the night we saw them as spirits. I believe that each of us (as a child of God) has come to earth with a portion of that divine inheri-tance that I witnessed in my children. Some may find that a little overwhelming, but I find it comforting to know where we have come from and what we yet have the potential to achieve.

Chapter Five

A VOICE FROM HEAVEN

*I*t was a bright, beautiful day. There were no clouds, just crystal blue skies in Provo, Utah. It seemed like heaven was smiling down on me and the thirty thousand plus who were attending Education Week at Brigham Young University (BYU).

It was August 20, 1992, and I was feeling sheer elation. The motivational classes I had attended since arriving at the BYU campus earlier in the week had radically recharged my batteries.

I was walking to the Marriott Center to meet a friend and enjoy another inspirational lecture. The only things that filled my mind were how glorious the day was, how much I was learning, and how great my next class was going to be. It was no wonder there was not a cloud in the sky; I was quite certain I was walking on any clouds that were around!

Then, as I walked to my next class, I was thrown a surprising spin. From inside my head, a male voice that I was unfamiliar with spoke to me. The voice said, "You have a son, and you must find him." The voice was clear and quiet, peaceful yet direct. No words were wasted—the message was to the point, and the impact was profound. After the brief message, I was left shaking and unable to pull a logical sequence of thoughts together.

At the time I heard the voice, I was about halfway between the Wilkinson Center and the Marriott Center. After receiving the message, I kept walking. I was so shaken by both the after effects of hearing the voice and the message that it was difficult to be fully coherent of my surroundings for at least thirty minutes after I was spoken to. I think I walked toward the Marriott Center. If I ever got close, I'm fairly certain I never made it inside. For some time, I walked aimlessly trying to regroup.

After the message that left me trembling, the experience my husband, Greg, and I had shared in 1978 during the first three months of our marriage immediately came to mind. A question that I'd had for over fourteen years was now answered. As I aimlessly walked on the campus at Brigham Young University, I knew who the fifth spirit in the doorway was—he was the son that I was to find.

Eventually I made my way back to the dorms. In my shaken state, all I could think to do was call Greg. I wasn't sure how he was going to react, but I intuitively knew that I needed to talk to him. I knew that Greg would not be able to talk until he got home from work, so I called him sometime that Thursday evening.

When he answered and I said hello, he could tell that I was noticeably shaken and that something was wrong. He asked, "Are you okay?" I responded, "No, you're not going to believe what happened today." Greg said, "Tell me what's going on—did something bad happen?" I told him, "Nothing bad has happened, but something has really shaken me up. I . . . I need to tell you what happened to me this afternoon." I then proceeded to tell him about the male voice talking to me. I explained to him that as soon as the voice had finished speaking to me, I knew that the son that I was to find was the fifth spirit—the male spirit that had stood inside our bedroom doorway the night that he and our four biological children had appeared in our bedroom.

After relating the details of my experience, with a little trepidation, I asked Greg, "Do you believe me?" Without hesitating, Greg lovingly replied, "Yes, I feel the same thing. I feel the Spirit telling me that the son you have been told to find is the spirit we saw in our bedroom doorway." I then asked him, "What do you think we should do?" Greg said, "Just try to enjoy what is left of Education Week. There isn't anything we can do until you get home." Then, afraid that maybe time was a factor, I said, "Do you think I should try to come home early?" Greg said, "No, there is no reason to come home early. We will get things figured out when you get home."

My instincts proved correct. Talking to Greg helped me calm down substantially. I felt so grateful that Greg had felt the confirmation in his heart that what I had told him was true. It was important for me to know that I would have Greg's support and assistance as we searched for our next son.

Within a couple of days, I was home in Butte, Montana, researching the processes of adoption. I soon found that adoption is a very involved process.

Most adoptions occur because couples are unable to produce offspring of their own. We already had four children. I knew this presented an interesting challenge, but it did not deter me from believing that I was going to get a baby. I was thrilled that I was going to get another baby and equally excited that I was not going to have to endure nine months of morning sickness as a part of the process! I launched my search, convinced that not only was I going to get a baby but that because God was behind it all, the process would be accomplished quickly and easily. It would not be an understatement to say that I initially misunderstood many things concerning what it would take and what accomplishing our adoption would entail.

As I researched adoption requirements, I became concerned about the health requirements. I had been experiencing frequent bouts of severe headaches for several months. Both Greg and I worried that this might be a deterrent in an adoption, so we decided to delay the pursuit of our adoption for a couple of months and concentrate on getting my headaches resolved.

I pursued treatment for my headaches, and all the while, I kept having feelings of guilt that I was not doing enough to find my son.

A few months later, in October, Greg and I met some of our friends from Billings, Montana, at the LDS (Church of Jesus Christ of Latter-day Saints) temple in Idaho Falls, Idaho. We were looking forward to spending time in the temple and seeing our friends.

In addition to our "pending" adoption, we had several other matters of concern on our minds. Prior to traveling to the temple, we prayed that we would be blessed with a spiritual experience in the temple. We were hoping to resolve some of our more pressing concerns.

In the temple, we were enjoying a wonderful session with our friends. As we entered a room of the temple, the same male voice that I heard at Education Week spoke to me a second time. This time, the voice seemed to communicate some impatience, and although the first message was repeated, further instructions were also given. He said, "You have a son and you must find him. His name is Andrew. He is in Romania, and you must teach him his heritage."

Once again, as before, I was left trembling and no longer fully aware of my surroundings. However, unaware of the experience that I had just had, Greg was anxiously trying to get my attention from across the room. Despite my challenged attentiveness, he somehow succeeded in getting my attention just long enough to get me to join him and a small group in the room. Yet, even after I joined him, I continued to be mostly unaware of my surroundings.

Once we moved to the next room of the temple, I had the opportunity to relate to Greg what had just happened in the previous room. However, as I started to relate to Greg the communication that I had just received, I had yet another experience. This caused me to pause, and Greg waited for my explanation. He had already seen that I was shaken, but now, as my next experience proceeded, he could see in my face and tell by the way that I stopped talking abruptly that something more was going on.

As I stood there, it felt as though the top of my head was painlessly opened and into me was poured the feelings of a mother for this son that I was to find. Those feelings started at the top of my head and continued to fill me until they reached my toes.

As soon as my experience was over and I regained some semblance of composure, I explained to Greg what had just been communicated to me in the previous room of the temple and what had happened just moments ago as I had stood next to him.

Previous to this experience, I had looked forward to having another child. However, until those feelings were poured into me, I had not had the same feelings for him that I had for my four birth children. After the feelings were poured into me, he was mine. Immediately, I had all of the same emotional attachments for this son that I had for my other children.

Looking for my son now took on an entirely different perspective.

At once, it felt as though this son had somehow been taken from my arms instead of feeling like I was looking for an unknown stranger. I felt as though I would never feel whole again until he was found.

Only a short time later, receiving those feelings of attachment to my son began to feel like a mean trick. Searching had been so much easier when I had not felt so emotionally attached to him.

After my temple experience, I had more clues to utilize in my adoption search, but receiving those specifics provided some of their own challenges. I was no longer looking for a nameless baby boy. I was now looking for a baby boy named Andrew who was in Romania. What little I knew about adoption thus far told me that eyebrows would certainly be raised if I approached an adoption agency with my story. I was concerned that most people would think that what I needed was a straitjacket rather than a child.

I felt that my best bet was to find a Christian international adoption agency. I thought that someone with religious beliefs would be much more inclined to listen instead of laugh. I looked up Christian adoption agencies on the internet and started making phone calls. During one call to an agency on the East coast, a man didn't exactly laugh; instead he asked me if I knew what I was asking for. In a cynical tone of voice, he said that I had a better chance of finding a needle in a haystack. He told me to give him a call once I found my child and then he would be happy to help me. I had already been shot down several times by the time I talked to this man, so I wasn't really in the mood for what he had to say. I needed help finding my child. I didn't need an explanation of the odds of my success and so, with more than a hint of frustration in my voice, I told him that this endeavor was not my idea. I told him that if it had been left to me, I would not have even thought to adopt. I emphasized that it was Heavenly Father who was directing this adoption and that I had to believe that God was more than capable of finding this needle in the haystack. His only response to my words of retribution was to abruptly end our phone call.

Searching for Andrew was a lonely and frustrating experience. Throughout my search, I was selective about who I shared my story with. The details of my experiences were generally shared with only close and trusted friends. They were shared with others only as necessary. I knew that few people could relate to the experiences that I'd had.

This became obvious to me when some of my closest friends that I had chosen to share my story with had difficulty understanding. They often would say something to the effect that I sure must have a lot of faith because they weren't sure that they could do the same thing. I hated those kinds of remarks (even from well-meaning friends). The search for my son had nothing to do with faith. My search was all about knowledge. And what I knew was this: Heaven had spoken and had poured the feelings of a mother into me for this child that I was to find and my heart was never going to let me stop searching until I found my son. There was no faith involved—just a lot of heartache.

Chapter Six

THE SEARCH

The iron curtain of Eastern Europe had come down a few years previous to my experience of being told to find Andrew. Until my focus turned toward Romania, I had not realized the plight of the people and countries of Eastern Europe. I was also not aware that many US citizens were looking to welcome orphaned children from those countries into their homes. Initially, people who were looking to adopt were able to travel to many of those countries and adopt children without the aid of adoption agencies. Romania was a popular destination for many such couples looking to adopt.

Relating my story to some friends led me to make contact with a Romanian man by the name of Dragos.* Dragos had served as an interpreter for several LDS (Mormon) couples who had traveled to Romania to adopt children without the aid of an adoption agency.

As I dialed Dragos's phone number for the first time, I kept praying, "Please let him be willing to help me. *Pleeeease* let me be able to understand him. Please, please, please let the Spirit communicate to him the truth of what I am about to tell him." Dragos answered the phone and greeted me in Romanian. For a brief moment, I thought I was doomed—I didn't speak a word of Romanian. "Do you speak English?" I asked. "Yes" was his reply. I then continued, "Do you have a few minutes that I can talk to you? I have been in contact with some people you helped to adopt children in Romania. They gave me your phone number and thought that you might be able to help me."

"What do you have in mind?" was Dragos's reply. I responded, "Well, first, I think I need to explain what I am trying to do and why I am hoping that you might be able to help me." Seeming somewhat interested, Dragos said, "Give me your information." I continued, "Well, it is my understanding that you helped several couples adopt children in Romania and that as you did so, several times you received inspiration that helped you procure documents and make contacts that ultimately ended up being critical in getting those adoptions accomplished."

"Yes," he replied.

"Well, if I understand correctly, you had never had those types of experiences before you helped with those adoptions, and as a result of those experiences with being guided by the Spirit, you joined the LDS church, right? I asked.

"Yes" was again his reply. I then started to explain, "I'm not sure where to begin, but I have had what many would consider an unusual experience. You see, I have been told that I am to find a son named Andrew who is in Romania."

I then related to Dragos my first experience of being told to find Andrew when I was at Brigham Young University for Education Week, and my second experience of being told to find Andrew, which occurred in the temple.

I then told him, "I don't know where Andrew is. I only know that he is in Romania. I don't have a lot of financial resources, yet I need to find a way to search for Andrew. I don't know if you would be willing to make some phone calls for me or if you would be willing to help me, but I know that I need to have someone's help who understands being guided by the Spirit. I've already called the LDS mission for your area hoping that maybe some missionaries could help me from time to time, and I wrote a letter to the area authority for the LDS Church, and none of them can help me. Do you think that you might be willing to help me?" Dragos then said, "Most people in my country think that all Americans are rich, but I have friends in your country, and I know this is not the case. I have a few contacts in orphanages throughout my country. If you feel that you can be patient, as I travel on business to various areas of my country, I will check out the orphanages in those areas and see what I can find. I cannot make you any promises, but I will try to do what I can."

I then asked, "Do you need me to send you some money?" He responded, "We will not worry about you paying me any money for now unless I need to incur some expenses in helping you search. I understand the source that is guiding your search, and I have seen these things happen before."

Dragos then shared with me some of the undeniable experiences with inspiration and receiving heavenly nudges that he'd had in regard to a few of the adoptions he had helped with. Knowing of his experiences helped me to trust him. After we hung up, I felt confident that finding him was not a coincidence.

Initially I worked only with Dragos. Later, Dragos started doing work for an adoption agency in Utah called Wasatch International Adoptions. His friends Jack and Emily Jones* were a part of that agency. Eventually, Jack and Emily became familiar with the details of my search and assisted me in my efforts to find Andrew as well.

My familiarity with Romania prior to being told that Andrew was there was sketchy at best. The details that I learned as I searched for Andrew left me feeling frantic and unsettled. It seemed as though I went from knowing and hearing nothing to frequently seeing TV news and reading stories in magazines and newspapers reporting the abhorrent conditions that were present in Romanian orphanages. Those reports did nothing to comfort me. In fact, they made me feel like a rescuer in a straitjacket. I found it extremely difficult to know that my son could be one of those orphanage babies who no longer cried because no one responded when he did.

I took this matter frequently to God in prayer. I easily approached Him on this matter at least a dozen times a day. Most of the time my conversations with God took on the air of a spoiled brat; my attitude was mainly "you got me into this mess, and now it's time you got me out." I would impatiently insist that I needed to make sure that my son was okay. I consistently maintained that Andrew needed me and the care that *only* I could provide him with.

I have never been the kind of person who was inclined to make deals with God, but after a short time, my prayers in regard to Andrew sounded more like barter sessions than communications with Deity. Eventually, after deciding that the spoiled brat attitude was highly ineffective, I attempted to back off a bit and hand the matter over to God's hands. However, my success in that venture could be compared to letting a child hold onto the steering wheel of a vehicle while the driver still maintained a white knuckle grip. God would have been the child, and I would have been the driver with the white knuckles. Logically, I knew that I needed to hand over the control in this situation, but I couldn't get my emotions to let go. My brain kept telling me that the entire matter was in God's hands, but those feelings in my heart kept me acting and handling the entire matter like I was the whole search and rescue team. Despite my attempts to turn everything over to the "proper authority," emotionally, it felt like my child had been kidnapped. Unfortunately, I was too immature emotionally and spiritually to turn everything over and let God be my guide like I needed to.

After many months of frustrated searching, a good friend shared some profound advice with me. She'd had a rebellious teenage son, and although our situations were different, our feelings of wanting to be in charge—of determining the results in regard to our children— were very much the same. She shared with me what, for her, had been a pivotal point in her own prayers of agony. She explained that Heavenly Father had finally been able to penetrate her closed mind to communicate to her that her son was His son first, that He loved her son even more than she did, and that He was doing everything in His power to help him. She felt certain that Heavenly Father would want me to know that as well.

For some reason, my friend's words of counsel struck a chord with my heart, and I resolved to handle my concerns for the son whom I had never seen a bit more constructively. I still prayed for help many times daily, but my prayers were better behaved, and I truly made a sincere effort to be a better listener.

After many months of fruitless searching and finally acknowledging that the chances of finding my son *quickly* were remote, I remodeled my prayers again. I still asked to find him soon, but as much as I wanted to find him, I wanted even more for him to be okay. So I started asking that wherever Andrew was, someone would love him.

During my conversations with Dragos, I found out that those children who were in hospitals generally got better and received more personal care. Some children were even kept in the hospitals after they were well because of the attachments that hospital staff developed for them. I didn't want Andrew to be sick, but I couldn't help but hope and pray that Andrew was in a hospital so that he would have more personal attention and the love that he needed.

Then, approximately eighteen months after I was told to find Andrew, I had a dream. In the dream, I was shown the country of Romania, with the hands of a clock originating from the city of Brasov and extending approximately northward and eastward (about 12:00 and 3:00). The border of Romania that lay between those two clock hands was shown very boldly, as if to stand out from the rest of the country's borders.

In the dream, I was told that a little girl who was four years old was with Andrew, that she loved him very much, and that she took good care of him. I was told that her name was Diana.

Although I don't remember being told, after the dream, I knew that the children were very close.

Knowing that the little girl was with Andrew provided unbelievable comfort to me. I knew that more than anything, Andrew needed love. I would have never thought of another child as a caretaker and source of love, but Heavenly Father had. Both of my daughters had been the "little mommy" type. I knew that a four-year-old probably couldn't diaper a baby with a lot of proficiency, but she would have lots of time and she would have lots of love. I couldn't help but send lots of thanks and tears of joy heavenward to Heavenly Father for providing someone for my son.

From that time forward, we started searching for both children. We knew they would be together. We did not know if Diana would be available for adoption when we found them, but we knew that if she was, we wanted to keep the children together. We hoped to be able to adopt them both. I prayed many times to know if Diana was Andrew's sister or a close friend, but it took an extended period of time before I was given that answer.

Once I knew of Diana's presence with Andrew, I immediately forwarded that information to Dragos. I also told Dragos about seeing the country of Romania with the clock hands at about 12:00 and 3:00. At that point, I thought that I was being shown where the children were. I thought that they would be somewhere in the area of Romania that lay northeast of Brasov, somewhere between the clock hands. Now in retrospect, I think that my belief that I was being shown where they were was accurate. However, the clock hands told only part of the story. I believe that the border of Romania that was shown so boldly was pointing me toward the actual land of their birth.

I didn't know Andrew's age, but I assumed that he had been born when I had first been told to find him. However, I knew Diana's age, so, keeping her age in mind, we looked for a little girl and a toddler who had a very close relationship with each other.

Soon after my experience in the Idaho Falls temple, we had a home study done. We decided to have an adoption agency by the name of Intercountry Adoptions in Bozeman, Montana, do our home study. We knew that in order to adopt, a home study needed to be done by an agency licensed in the state of Montana.

We were eager to have the home study done and hesitant to share the details that were prompting our adoption. Initially, we thought there might be a way to skirt those issues, but that was only wishful thinking. A social worker by the name of Judy was assigned to our family. Judy was very kind and personable, and she had lots of questions.

As we had grudgingly anticipated, Judy questioned why, in addition to specifying the gender of the child we wanted, we were also particular about his name and country of origin. It was obvious that our specificity had aroused Judy's curiosity. Deciding that it was only going to raise greater concerns if we remained silent about the experiences that were precipitating our adoption, we chose to share our story.

After listening to me explain how we had come to pursue our adoption and why we needed to make sure that we found a boy by the name of Andrew who was from Romania, Judy said, "From your story, it is obvious that Andrew is a very special child. How are you going to tell Andrew that he was chosen by God, and how are you going to explain to your biological children that he is more special than they are?

As I thought about my reply to her, a message from God came to me. I looked at Judy and repeated the message I had just been given. "Andrew is not more special than any of my other children. God loves each and every one of His children the same, and if it were necessary, He would do the same for them as well." As I relayed the message to Judy that I had just been given, I felt amazing warmth fill my heart, confirming to me the truth of the inspiration I had just received.

Three years after completing our interviews with Judy, our first home study expired. However, our search for Andrew and Diana continued. After a time, Dragos seemed to grow weary of my phone calls and insisted that I only call Jack and Emily Jones. Eventually, Jack and Emily grew tired of my phone calls as well.

They would suggest that maybe Andrew was not his name, that maybe that was only God's name for my son but not his earthly name. They would kindly insist that all possibilities had been exhausted. After I realized that they were no longer committed to helping me, I gave up contacting them altogether. Much later, I found out that Dragos had long given up searching for Andrew. I was told that he had become convinced that Andrew was a figment of my imagination and that searching for him was a waste of his time. I can understand the frustrations that Dragos and the Joneses had—I had more than a few myself. Yet I knew what I had been told and I knew that I had not been given an updated message from God. I didn't know what else to do but to use the information that I had been given and keep trying to find my child.

Every now and then, as frustrations built up and no relief seemed imminent, I would shake my fist at heaven and let God know that He had been unfair to me when He had given me the feelings of a mother for the son I had never met or held. Yet, I have to confess that even in those moments of frustration, I always knew why those feelings had been given to me, and I knew that it would be because of those feelings that my son would be found.

From time to time, Chad, my oldest son, would come up to me and ask, "Mom, have you gotten any closer to finding Andrew?" My answer was usually something like, "No, but I am hopeful that a new contact I have made will help us." So rarely was there any breakthrough or news that I often felt that my replies sounded like a broken record—the same information repeated over and over. Still, his inquiries had a way of instilling in me the feeling that he believed in me and that he knew that the time would come when we would find Andrew. His confidence always had a way of buoying my spirits.

*Names have been changed to protect the privacy of those involved.

Chapter Seven

ANSWERED PRAYERS

*I*T had been over five years since my initial experience of being told to find Andrew. Hope was an important commodity to me, because after searching for Andrew for so long, I began to have doubts. I knew that my experiences had not been imagined, but I began to be convinced that somehow, somewhere along the way I had really blown the chance to find my son. I didn't know what I had done wrong, but I decided that it must have been really bad. I began to feel that God must have decided to give Andrew to someone else. During one of my prayers I relayed this concern. I told Heavenly Father that I apologized if I had done something wrong. I begged him to please let me know if Andrew had been given to someone else and that if that were the case, to please let my emotional bond to Andrew be removed.

After my prayer pleading to know if I had done something wrong or if Andrew had been given to someone else, no answer contrary to my original instructions was received. However, after searching for so long, I had reached a point emotionally that felt as if I was running on empty. It was an extremely difficult time for me. It didn't help that my lack of progress in finding the children had significantly reduced my reserves of hope.

Over the years that I searched for Andrew and Diana, I spent countless hours looking online at international adoption sites. Since I didn't know if Andrew and Diana were siblings or not, I would look at all possibilities. I looked for them individually and I looked for them together. I often worried that somehow, while looking online and elsewhere, I had passed them by. I kept my eyes and ears open to any and all leads. I continually looked for opportunities to talk to anyone and everyone who might prove to be a lead or guide me to a useful contact.

Because I was not given any divine communication letting me know that my search needed to end, I continued to search online, and I continued my efforts to find some new lead or some new contact who would bring me closer to my son. In spite of being depleted emotionally, I continued to feel a strong emotional bond with my unfound son. And I continued to pray many times daily that I would be guided to find both Andrew and Diana, the little girl we hoped would be ours as well.

A short time after my prayer asking Heavenly Father if He had changed His mind about letting me have Andrew, a friend told me about her friend who'd had an experience somewhat similar to mine. Her friend had recently found and adopted a child. I quickly got her friend's phone number and made a call to her, thinking that maybe just talking to someone who had experienced a happy ending might buoy my spirits. I knew I needed some recharging. At that point, I was so frustrated with the dismal results of my "search and rescue" efforts that I often had the thought that if I ever got to have Andrew, he would be an adult by the time I did.

As I'd hoped, the conversation I had with my new contact turned out to be both comforting and informational; her adoption experience had been based mainly on impressions, but we both knew through some sort of personal revelation that we needed to seek for and find a child that was to be made a part of our family. During our conversation, I asked what adoption agency she had used. She told me that her adoption had been accomplished through Wasatch International Adoptions—the same agency that Jack and Emily Jones were a part of. She didn't know Jack and Emily, but she had nothing but praise for a woman by the name of Micki Elmer, who had helped her and her husband. She strongly encouraged me to contact Micki and share my story with her. She felt that if anyone would or could help me, it would be Micki.

I called Micki that very same day. My conversation with Micki began almost apologetically. (By that time I had experienced a fair amount of rejection.)

"Hi Micki. I was given your name by a friend of mine. Do you have a few minutes that I could talk to you? My friend told me how you helped her and that she knew you would truly listen to me. She said you have helped many people who have been impressed that there was a child that needed to be part of their family."

Micki kindly said, "Yes, I have been involved with a few people who've had impressions that another child was supposed to be a part of their family. I'm currently involved with Wasatch Adoptions, and I work with families that are trying to adopt."

I then started into my story. "I hope you won't mind, but I need to share some information with you in order for you to understand what I'm trying to accomplish." I then related to her my experience of being told to find Andrew, my contact with Dragos, and all other paths I had pursued in my efforts to find Andrew.

When I finished relating my story, I asked, "Do you think you would be willing to help me try to find Andrew?"

She then told me, "I want you to know that as you told me about your experiences, I felt goose bumps go up and down my spine, and I knew that what you were telling me was true. I have seen many miracles happen as families were guided to the child that was to be a part of their family. I don't know how it's going to happen or how long it's going to take, but I feel that somehow we are going to be able to find Andrew and the little girl who is with him."

I then asked, "So what do I need to do?"

Micki said, "I think we need to make a fresh start. I think it would be best if we proceed as though nothing had yet been done to find Andrew. Will that be okay with you?"

Feeling a surge of excitement, I said, "That would be great. I appreciate so much that you are willing to help me!"

"Not a problem, I will contact my people in Romania and have them see what they can find. If we need to, we can also do some checking in Moldova too. Did you know that Moldova was once part of Romania?

"Yes," I said, "We've actually made efforts to search there but with no success."

"Just remember," Micki said, "I have seen Heavenly Father guide this type of process many times, and while I don't want to get your hopes up, just know that we will do all that we can to find Andrew and Diana."

I hung up with Micki feeling more hopeful than I had in months.

Once Micki was on board in our effort to find Andrew and Diana, we essentially started from scratch just as she had suggested. Micki made contact with her people in Romania and Moldova, and they looked through all of their records of adoptable children in those countries. Nothing was found that looked promising.

Micki next asked me if I would be okay with searches in Bulgaria, Yugoslavia, and Hungary, countries that bordered Romania. Each time, I gave the go ahead. Both Micki and I thought that with the time that had passed, it might be possible that the children had been moved to a different location. Discouraged from years of fruitless searching, I didn't expect any positive results. Yet I knew that I needed to be optimistic and have faith in our efforts to find the children. However, those additional searches did not produce any results.

After about a year of unsuccessfully searching all of Romania and the surrounding countries, Micki *gently* asked me if I would give her permission to make contact with all of the countries that her agency did adoptions in. She seemed to understand that the years of unsuccessful searching had taken a toll. After I gave her permission to proceed, she told me that I could expect her contact for Russia to call me within a few days to let me know what she had.

When Danae, Micki's contact, got in touch with me, she had me go to a secure website and look at the pictures of children there. After looking through the pictures on the website, I called Danae.

"Danae, I went to the secure website today like you instructed. I looked through all of the pictures, and I didn't see anything there."

"Are you sure there was nothing there that looked promising?" asked Danae.

"Yes, I was really hopeful that I would find something, but I'm just not seeing anyone who looks like it could be one of them." I replied.

She added, "You know, I just noticed that two children—I think a brother and a sister—have just been added to the list for our Russian program. If I remember right, the name of the little boy was Andre. I don't remember the name of the little girl. Would you be interested in their information?"

The name Andre immediately got my attention. It is the European form of the name Andrew.

"Yes." I quickly asked, "What else do you know about them?"

She then looked through her paperwork so that she could verify the information she had on them.

"It shows here that they are a brother and a sister. The little boy's name is Andre just as I thought, and the little girl's name is Dina. Dina is eight years old, and Andre is six.

When she told me the ages of the children, I really started to get excited. (The ages were right on target.)

I excitedly told Danae, "The name of the little boy that I am trying to find is Andrew, and the name of the little girl who is with him is Diana. I can't believe that their names are so close to the names that I am looking for. Andre would be translated into English as Andrew, right?"

"Yes. Would you like us to email you a picture of them?"

I quickly responded, "Yes, I would definitely like that. How soon can you send them?"

She told me, "I'll have to tell the office that has their file to send them to you. I will call the office and have them send the pictures to you tomorrow." Then she said, "By the way, do you have a current home study?

"No," I explained, "After our first home study expired, we were told not to do another until we found the children."

She then said, "Well I don't want to get your hopes up, but I have a feeling that something is happening in your search for your children, and you might want to think about getting another home study done." My heart rate picked up at this comment.

They attempted to email us the pictures of the children the very next day, but the pictures never came through. After verifying the correct email address, another attempt to email their pictures was planned for the following day. Despite the problems with the first email, my entire family and I began to feel as if the pendulum was finally swinging our way and that the time had come to complete our family. The next day's activities had already been planned, but we found that everyone could be home at about 5:00 that evening. The following day, we all gathered around the computer monitor to open the email. As the picture slowly revealed itself line by line, I knew I was seeing the faces of my children. I was not the only one who knew—my whole family knew.

The emotional impact on each of us was overwhelming. Tissues could not keep up with our tears. Six and a half years of waiting, unrealized hopes, worries, and heartfelt prayers were unleashed. We would look at the computer screen and cry and then we would look at each other and cry some more. I suspect that our reactions were not a lot different from that of a family seeing pictorial evidence that family members had survived after being separated by war or a devastating natural disaster.

After searching for them for so many years and worrying that somehow I had missed them, I was surprised how quickly and easily I recognized them. I had never seen them before, yet their faces were amazingly familiar.

After hugging, crying, jumping, and celebrating our joy, our first move was to call Micki to let her know that we had found the children. Poor Micki, we were crying so hard when we called her that she thought something really horrible had happened. We soon convinced her that our tears were tears of rejoicing, and then we cried and laughed and celebrated the rest of the evening.

Later that night, when everyone had finally settled down, I let my thoughts wander through all of the challenges and obstacles that had led up to this wonderful, emotional day. Seeing the faces of Andre and Dina download on our computer monitor drove home several lessons for me. I realized that I needed to work to internalize the truths that are revealed to me by Heavenly Father with greater intent. Though I had completely believed in the task that Heavenly Father had set before me—the task of finding Andrew—I had not actively allowed any of my focus to see the big picture as it had been given to me. Our family was planned well before my husband and

I or any of our children ever entered our mortal bodies. Seeing our children before they were born was the first piece of evidence. In addition to seeing him as a spirit, each message that I received concerning Andrew told me that I had a son. Yet Andrew was not born until two and a half years after I was told to find him. He was not physically present on earth; nevertheless, Heavenly Father considered him my son.

I also realized my need to acknowledge that Heavenly Father was completely in charge of the search to find Andrew and Diana despite my prolonged unwillingness to recognize that fact. Notwithstanding my anxious prayers, pleading, frustrations, and impatience, Heavenly Father's original plan for the final additions to be made to our family was carried out. If I'd had more faith in God and His methods, everyone concerned would have benefited. I still have questions as to why events needed to transpire as they did, but despite those questions, I have no reservations that there were valid and profound reasons for events to transpire as they did.

We soon got further details on the children. They had just been added to the list of adoptable children for the country of Russia. They had been in an orphanage for six months after having been removed from their birth parents. (At the time, Russian law stipulated that children could not be made available for adoption until they had been a ward of the state for at least six months.)

The name of the little girl was Dina (pronounced Deena). The English translation of her name is Diana. Dina was eight and a half years old. We were initially told that Andre was six years old, but when we received the paperwork with the children's health details, we found that he was actually only three and a half. I was surprised by this detail but grateful as well. It meant I had only missed three and a half years with Andre instead of six.

Chapter Eight

THE TRIP TO RUSSIA

*I*f ever there had been a time since I had started searching for Andrew and Diana that I could have been content with not finding them, it was those last months of 1998, but such was Heavenly Father's way of answering my prayers and helping me grow.

At the time we found Andrew and Diana, our ordinarily busy life was busier than I had ever known it. Our four teenagers and their extracurricular activities kept our family hopping. Additionally, we were juggling the overwhelming demands of running a business and being self-employed, purchasing a second business and undergoing training for that purchase, and preparing for the wedding of our oldest daughter—which, for me, included sewing the wedding dress. Finding the children created two more irons in the fire, refinancing our home to pay for their adoption and compiling all the paperwork necessary for two international adoptions.

Handling all that life threw at me in those busy months was truly a miracle. By 1998, I had been experiencing migraine head-aches 24-7 for several years, so it was amazing that I was able to function at all, let alone keep up with all of the important demands in my life.

I was briefly hopeful that we would get a two for one deal—one set of papers for two children. Unfortunately for me, governments tend to be extremely finicky about adoption paperwork and are not terribly concerned about the inconvenience that duplication of effort creates.

First on the adoption agenda was getting another home study done. Our second home study was handled by Catholic Social Services. No difficult questions to answer with the second home study—we had already found the children!

I compiled a large notebook full of all the paperwork and legal documents that would be required for our adoption. Everything from health records and specialized packing lists to apostilled copies of our birth certificates and marriage license ended up in my notebook. (Though we already had copies of our birth certificates and marriage license, apostilled copies verifying that the notaries who had notarized them were in good standing at the time the documents were notarized had to be obtained from the state capitals of the states we were born and married in.)

The Immigration and Naturalization Service (INS) required that fingerprints be submitted to the FBI for verification that no criminal records existed for Greg and me; local authorities had to verify we had no criminal charges or history. Three letters of recommendation had to be procured from friends and passports had to be obtained.

By the time all of the paperwork for the adoption was compiled and completed, I decided that it would have been easier to endure morning sickness for nine months!

We hoped that we would be able to travel to Russia in January 1999, but because of court closures, the courts in Russia did not allow us to complete our adoption until April 1999.

The children were in an orphanage in a small village on the east coast of Russia when we found them. The adoption proceedings were conducted in Vladivostok, Russia, a large coastal city on the southeastern tip of the country.

Packing was a challenging ordeal. We had to maximize the use of the luggage we were allowed. In addition to packing for ourselves, we had to pack clothing for the children, which necessitated inclusion of winter coats and all the clothing they would need for a two-week period. Additionally, we were told to bring our own supply of food, so all of our edible provisions needed space in our suitcases as well.

The Kosovo conflict was raging as we found the children and prepared to travel to Russia. As a result, a few members of our family tried to talk us into waiting until Kosovo was resolved, fearing for our safety while in Russia. Other family members, who already thought our family was large enough, tried to talk us out of adopting altogether. Although we did not feel Kosovo would have an impact on our adoption or our trip to Russia, it was probably one of the reasons we were instructed to bring attire that would enable us to blend in rather than be easily identified as Americans. (Despite our best efforts to follow their instructions, we stuck out like a sore thumb, and we could easily identify other Americans we met on the streets just by looking at them.)

Our two-and-a-half-week trip to Russia commenced on April 11, 1999. We drove to Spokane, Washington, and flew from Spokane to Seattle, where we caught a flight on the Russian airline Aeroflot from Seattle to Vladivostok. We flew out of Seattle with a single mom from Utah who was adopting a thirteen-month-old baby boy.

Greg and I were a little nervous about flying to Russia, but that nervousness increased dramatically when our plane made its first landing on Russian soil. Our first landing was made in Khabarovsk, Russia. We were surprised to see that the airport seemed more like an abandoned military base. Old weathered airplanes with questionable functionality dotted the tarmac. Our initial astonishment turned to tension as armed men in military type uniforms drove up to our airplane and one of their commanders barked harsh words at the flight attendants and demanded possession of their passports. Our first touchdown in Russia made it painfully clear to us that while on Russian soil, we would not have the same freedoms that we were accustomed to in the United States.

Our second landing was just outside the city of Vladivostok, the destination for our adoption. Though friendlier than our initial landing, going through customs verified our initial impressions that as foreigners in their country, we were not welcome visitors.

The area in and around Vladivostok was obviously suffering from severe economic difficulties. It appeared that the city had once been a prosperous seaside resort area. However, half-constructed buildings, deteriorating from neglect, and the deplorable state of their streets communicated a city that had been suffering economically for quite some time.

We were greeted by our interpreter once we were processed through customs. She worked for our adoption agency and provided assistance to us and to others who had come to Vladivostok to adopt children. Her first order of business was to get us settled in our rooms at the Vladivostok Motor Inn. From there, she arranged for Greg and me to go to the transitional orphanage to meet our children for the first time.

We had been instructed to bring games and other types of entertainment with us that would enable us to interact with the children without requiring verbal communication. The children spoke no English, and we spoke virtually no Russian. Therefore, Greg decided to bring a ball with us.

As the children were brought into the room to meet us, it was so hard to keep my emotions under control. I so fervently wanted to race to them, grab them up in my arms, and not let go for a very long time. However, circumstances dictated that our first meeting be handled with a gentler display of emotions. Nine-year-old Dina was shy and understandably a little fearful of the prospective parents she was being introduced to. Four-year-old Andre was much less reserved, and he was delighted when Greg attempted to play ball with him.

As Dina, our interpreter, and I watched Andre play ball with Greg, I could tell that it made Dina happy to see Andrew have fun. While we watched them play, the interpreter turned to me and said, "Andre and Dina are very close." She further explained, "You probably don't know this, but Dina has been like a mother to Andre. In fact, he does not call his sister Dina but calls her mama Dina."

I caught my breath as she iterated what had already been provided to me years before through personal revelation the night that I had been told that Dina was with Andre. As my mind fast-forwarded from the night of my dream through all the events that led to us being in that room with our children, all I could do was shake my head at her and say, "I know."

The next day, we were able to meet with the children again. The moment that Dina saw me, she came running, wrapping her arms around me crying "Mama! Mama!" She did not want to let go of me. While Dina and I cried, two little girls about the same age as Dina vied for Greg's attention, giving him presents and begging him to take them with us. Andrew was not feeling well and was in the dormitory resting on his bed. We were allowed to take the children with us at the conclusion of our second visit. They were with us for our remaining time in Russia.

Once the children were in our possession, I felt a great sense of relief, and I also had feelings of anxiousness. I looked forward to incorporating the children into our family, yet, at the same time, I worried about how the children were going to handle being taken away from everything that was familiar to them.

Despite the language barrier, Greg and I were quickly able to pick up on many of the children's personality traits and several of their likes and dislikes. It was interesting to watch them interact with each other. They had a very close relationship, but they still had little squabbles with each other like most siblings do.

On April 15th, we went to court, and the children became ours. Our interpreter had emphasized that as we appeared before the judges, we were not to smile. We were to reflect a serious countenance. The reason being that laughing or smiling would be construed as making light of our adoption proceedings—an offense serious enough to cause our adoption to be denied.

As instructed, we did not laugh or smile, which was not difficult at all. The atmosphere of the courthouse seemed very ominous, so keeping a serious demeanor was an easy accomplishment. When our turn came, we were questioned by the adoption judges for several minutes and then spent several more anxious minutes waiting for their decision in the hallway outside. We were then brought back into the judge's room and given their affirmative decision which, to our surprise, was then followed by big smiles from the judges and expressions of their congratulations! As we turned to our interpreter with puzzled expressions on our faces, she told us that we could smile back at them.

The remainder of our time in Russia was spent doing a little bit of sightseeing and getting the passports for the children so that we could take them home with us. Once we had the necessary documents, our interpreter had to make a round trip flight across seven time zones from Vladivostok to Moscow to complete the work on the children's passports.

Once the children's passports were in hand, we were eager to get home to the rest of our family and get back to our normal lives. Our suitcases were considerably lighter, but we now had children in addition to our baggage to manage. Greg took Andrew through customs, and I took Dina. Things proceeded smoothly through the customs booth that Dina and I went through. Greg and Andrew encountered a customs clerk who apparently had some personal issues with US citizens adopting Russian children. She tried to claim that Andrew could not be allowed to leave the country because Greg's passport was from the United States and Andrew's passport was from Russia. She tried to take her argument up the chain of command, but everyone in customs knew that Andrew had been adopted and was now being taken to the United States by his adoptive parents. As she made her appeals to her superiors, her fellow workers would roll their eyes and shake their heads the moment she turned away from them—universal gestures that we readily recognized and easily communicated to us their feelings about their fellow employee's outrage.

Once on board our Aeroflot flight for the return flight home, the children and I were given the royal treatment by our flight attendants. The flight was fairly empty, so the flight attendants sent Greg toward the back of the plane and made beds for each of the children utilizing a full row of seats for each child. They then made sure I was next to the children and that my needs were taken care of as well.

For our first leg of the flight home, we flew from Vladivostok to Sakhalin Island, Russia. It would have seemed like an amazingly wonderful flight were it not for our landing on Sakhalin Island. Once we were on the ground, armed men had the entire plane disembark, and we were ushered into a building and locked in a room. Time seemed to crawl. Our inability to understand Russian and the country's recent history of communism easily enabled uncertainty and fear to invade our emotions. Guards with guns combined with vivid imaginations do little to calm troubled hearts. Though we never knew the reason for our incarceration in the room, it was with a sense of gratitude and relief that we boarded the plane once again.

A "note to self" was registered in my mind as we lifted off from Sakhalin Island—never ever take freedom for granted. I am always grateful for a safe landing, but I have never been more grateful than the moment we touched down on US soil in Anchorage, Alaska, on our return flight home. The ground was still cold and barren-looking around the airport in Anchorage that day in late April, but that US soil and all the freedoms that came with it had never looked so good or felt so wonderful under my feet. I truly wanted to get down on my knees and kiss the ground (a gesture that, prior to our trip to Russia, I thought was a little over the top when I had seen returning US military do it—but not anymore)!

Our trip to Russia certainly instilled in me an increased sense of patriotism, but the conclusion of our trip also brought with it a sense of lessons learned—not just from the trip itself but also from the entire experience that began the day I was told to find my son.

As I've reflected on those experiences, I've been reminded of God's hand in it all and His perfect precision in maneuvering the events just as they needed to occur.

We found Andrew and Diana the moment they became available for adoption. I believe that the timing involved was a complete manifestation of divine intervention. However, my first question in that regard was why I couldn't just have been told to find them once they were available. However, I knew the answer even before I asked the question. I knew I needed to have the learning experiences that my search provided me with. Heavenly Father does not construct our life's experiences with convenience in mind. He utilizes the experiences we have as opportunities for growth. If efficiency in getting the job done was Heavenly Father's primary concern, I *could* have been told to find Andrew at the time he and Dina became available for adoption. Additionally, God *could* have provided me with their location and all other pertinent data He wanted me to have. However, Heavenly Father is a master teacher. He is completely aware of both my shortcomings and my strengths. I am convinced that He used the experience of finding my children to further enhance my strengths and to provide me with opportunities to overcome my weaknesses.

I have learned from my experiences that we seldom have the

perfect and complete perspective that Heavenly Father has. Another lesson that I learned is that not only are our families planned prior to our being born but our ancestry is important as well. I do not claim to know all the reasons, but I know it is so.

Some may wonder why I was told that Andrew was in Romania since we found the children in Russia. I call that some of Heavenly Father's diversionary tactics. (Looking in Romania and its surrounding areas certainly kept me diverted until it came time to find them.) Yet there was no lie contained in my instruction that he was in Romania.

As Greg and I first analyzed my being told that Andrew was in Romania when we found him in Russia, it initially made no sense. Greg asked me several times if I had heard wrong when the voice spoke to me. He would ask me if the voice could have said Russia instead of Romania. I know without any reservations that I was told Romania. Knowing that Heavenly Father cannot lie, I searched for several years for the answer to why I was told that Andrew was in Romania. (Both children were adamant that they had never been in the country of Romania.) I received the answer about six years after our adoption was complete. The inspiration that I received told me that his mother was of Romanian descent and that because he had been in his mother, Andrew was "in" Romania. The children were found on the east coast of Russia. The distance between Romania and Southeastern Russia made that explanation seem somewhat unlikely. However, after a couple of conversations with people who have lived in Eastern Russia, it no longer seems far-fetched to me at all. As Joseph Stalin invaded the countries of Eastern Europe, he removed people from his conquered countries and sent them to various parts of Russia. Then he sent Russian citizens to live in those countries he had occupied to prevent the threat of uprisings. The Russians considered the people of Romania to be inferior. Many Romanians were sent to the east coast of Russia to work the gold, diamond, and coal mines—hard work that the Russians felt more appropriately belonged to the inferior Romanians. During one of my investigative conversations, I was told that those who are of Russian descent are easily recognizable. They are generally fair-skinned with features similar to Americans and Europeans of Germanic descent.

Andrew is fair-skinned with blond hair and blue eyes. He looks like a Russian. Dina has an olive complexion, with dark brown hair and brown eyes. Both of the children have said that Andrew looks like their birth father and that Dina looks like their birth mother. That being the case, their mother has the physical characteristics of someone of Romanian descent and not the physical attributes of someone of Russian descent.

Andrew was in "Romania" when I was told to find him. His mother of Romanian descent still carried the egg that would eventually form his mortal body. Andrew was not born until two and a half years after I was told to find him. Yet, as I was told and our Russian interpreter verified, Dina loved him very much and had taken care of him.

It is clear to me that from God's perspective, Andrew did not have to be born or even be a growing fetus in order for him to be considered my son. The only criterion was that it had to have been planned already in heaven.

All of these things have been lessons for me—some of them lessons learned after the fact. I was never given the exact steps that would be needed to find the children. I was obviously expected to act for myself. Yet I know that Heavenly Father knew that as long as I made a sincere effort to find my son, all the right contacts would be made, and when the time was right, the job would be accomplished.

Chapter Nine

PRAYERS AND PERSONAL REVELATION

*O*ne of the great lessons I have learned is that God is always there for me—not always with the answer I want but with the answer I need. He is perfect, and my lack of understanding does not change that or limit Him in any way.

Once answers from God are received, I have learned it is my job to accept them and to act upon them. In most instances, I continue to feel reassurances in my heart that an answer is correct. However, there have been times when answers have not been strong or overwhelming. Self-doubt or doubt on the part of others has sometimes led me to seek the same answer twice. At times I have been denied my request for a second response. I have found that this is Heavenly Father's way of letting me know that I have already been answered and I need to pay closer attention the first time.

As a result, I have finally learned to write down my spiritual impressions. Writing them down is much more durable and long-lasting than my memory. Many times, inspiration that I have recorded in my journal reteaches me or helps me with a new situation.

I have found that it is important that, every so often, I take time to read through the words of guidance that I have received and recorded. I never walk away from those experiences without feeling refreshed, reeducated, strengthened, and determined to do better.

The power of prayer is undeniably real to me, and it blesses my life each and every day. Prayer and personal revelation walk hand in hand with each other. Rarely is one without the other. I believe that the simplicity of prayer and personal revelation is a manifestation of God's hand in the entire process. People often make communication and relationships more complicated than they need to be. Heavenly Father, on the other hand, keeps communication with His children brilliantly simple.

My personal experience has seen several consistencies manifested:

In almost all instances, I am the one who needs to initiate contact.

When I make a request for information, I am expected to listen for the answer. The listening I refer to does not always refer to hearing but means I need to have a receptive heart so that I recognize my answer in whatever form it comes.

My answers come according to God's timetable and not my own.

God's answers to me will always be based on His perfect understanding of my circumstances and His love for me rather than on my mortal understanding or desires.

I need to record the answers that I receive. Those answers are personal revelation, and I too easily forget what I receive if I don't write it down.

I believe in the whisperings of the heart. Being taken back to premortality only confirmed what my heart had already told me:

Heavenly Father loved me, knew me personally, had a plan for my life, and would be a continual source of strength and guidance *if* I allowed Him to be.

Not just my children, but my entire family was planned in advance.

The heart, when in tune with heavenly sources, only communicates truth.

The opportunities afforded me by the life and Atonement of my Savior Jesus Christ was real and not imagined.

I could trust the "whisperings" my heart had received regarding those feelings that could not be humanly proved but that consistently and lovingly manifested themselves as more than just a whimsical thought. An example of this is my feeling that I had known my husband Greg before this life and that God was personally aware of me and loved me.

In my youth, my prayers were often mechanical. They were not memorized prayers, but if a person could have listened in on a regular basis, they might have guessed they were. Now, because of my experiences and the knowledge I have gained, my personal prayers are conversations. Each is an opportunity to check in with my Heavenly Father, who loves and understands me perfectly. They are opportunities to be taught and strengthened by that wonderfully perfect Being who is in possession of the "crystal ball" to my life.

Because I have always known Satan is real, there once was a time when I hesitated to make my personal prayers verbal. I didn't want Satan hearing what I had to say. I didn't want him knowing *even more* of my personal weaknesses. At some point in my life, someone was kind enough to share with me that they believed that spoken prayers brought strength to the relationship between our Father and His children in a way that silent prayers were unable to accomplish. I gave that theory a try, and I have been grateful ever since.

Spoken personal prayers in some intangible yet tangible way have strengthened me and strengthened my relationship with my Creator. I believe that I am able to focus more, and I feel greater harmony when I pray vocally.

My prayers might once have been compared to a checklist: everything I knew I should be grateful for, everything I truly was grateful for, and a really long list of everything I wanted. Except in times of need, I did not consider prayer to be anything more than a daily obligation.

I am so thankful that God has been willing to teach me that prayer can be so much more than an obligation or a mechanical list of thanks and needs.

Sometimes my prayers are nothing more than expressions of gratitude: reporting a success I've had, expressing my love, giving thanks for a hurdle He has helped me to overcome, voicing words of wonder in regard to His perfection and creations and His ever-inspiring ability to deal with that all too consistently disjointed figure I call *me*. Other times I have deep concerns I need to address. Those concerns include people problems, health, world and community issues, and desires for greater understanding.

Both types of prayer are most successful when I take time to listen. Some call it meditating. I prefer to think of it as offering my Heavenly Father a chance to answer.

Some may think it odd that I would want to listen at the end of a prayer that simply expresses thanks. However, I am always blessed when I do. Though I do not ask for guidance in my prayers of gratitude, I often receive answers nonetheless, and most important, I always walk away from those moments with reinforced knowledge in my heart that though I am one in several billions (or more), He loves me, He knows me individually, and I am worth His effort.

Even though I was young when I was taught that effective prayer needs to be a two-way street, it still took me many years and many experiences to really understand that listening for a reply is an essential part of the prayer process. Throughout that learning process, I have also learned to be specific with my questions.

Answers to my prayers are not always immediate; it can take days, weeks, or even years to get an answer. Often, my answers come in unexpected ways. Sometimes I am told yes, sometimes no. Sometimes I am directed that I need to work harder to find the solution; sometimes I am told that I need to be easier on myself or let up a little. A few times, I have been directed that the answers I seek will have to wait until I return to God's presence. I have even been told that an answer I seek belongs to someone else.

For me, prayer is a door that, when opened, makes available to me anything and everything that I *truly* need; however, it is a door that *relies on me* to be opened.

My ability to receive answers is always helped by an understanding of true and false voices. I never receive an answer contrary to God's commandments nor am I ever relieved of my ability to choose. However, when I am glued to the television or I allow my life to become too frenzied, I rarely get the answers I am seeking. I have found that it is important to schedule time to reflect and make sure I am spiritually fed. When I do, my answers come with much greater frequency and ease.

Often, reflecting upon previous answers that I have received or upon past spiritual experiences has provided me with additional enlightenment. For example, immediately after my experience of being taken back to premortality, I didn't know who the angel was who had taken me from my body and escorted me back to heaven. Yet some details struck me as odd. The entire time that I had been with the angel he had seemed to make a deliberate effort to keep his face turned away from me. He had directed my attention from one scene to another but never toward himself. And somehow, I knew that this angel loved me very much. So why didn't he want me to look at him? He had appeared to be in his late twenties or early thirties; but then, so had our children when they had appeared to my husband and me. Our spirits do not show age like our mortal bodies, so utilizing age as an identifying factor wasn't helpful.

I thought about my angel for several months before I finally decided to ask who he was. Once my question was petitioned, my answer was immediate—the angel was my grandfather.

It was amazing to me how much everything made sense once I knew who my angel was. I love my grandfather so much that if I would have known that it was him, he never would have been able to divert my attention away from him and toward the things I needed to see. His keeping his face away from me had been a loving gesture; a gesture that had literally saved my life. Yet, knowing that it was my grandfather explained why I had known that my angel loved me. My grandfather, who had shown so much love to me during his mortal life, had made use of yet another opportunity to express his love. Yet, had I not reflected on that experience I might not have ever known that my grandfather had been my rescuer.

✳ ✳ ✳

If there is one thing that prayer and personal revelation have taught me, it is that I am an imperfect amateur with greater desires than I have ability. Many times, Heavenly Father has had to repeatedly prod me with small measures just to help me understand something relatively simple. Other times the answers or direction from God have been more complex. Such was the case when I was told that Andrew was in Romania and I found him, instead, in Russia. I was given correct information, but I did not understand and was not meant to understand the application of that information until much later.

When my husband and I went through the red tape of adoption, the scrutiny was intense: letters had to be submitted by friends attesting to our abilities as responsible parents, visits were made to our home by social workers, our children were interviewed and questioned, the FBI had to clear our fingerprints, and in addition to these things, the paperwork seemed endless.

That was the easy part of our adoption. For the six and a half years that I searched for Andrew and Diana, I prayed, and I prayed, and I prayed. I knew how to pray with fervency, with intensity, with real desire, but I didn't really know how to pray. I would try occasionally to listen for answers, but I mainly provided God with instructions on what I expected Him to do for me. Most if not all of my prayers were selfish and self-centered and lacked an understanding of God's ability and desire to direct me, not only for my own good but also for the good of those around me. My prayers reflected my inability and unwillingness to place my wholehearted faith in God. Because of my wayward approach to praying, I made the entire process much more difficult than it needed to be.

I had an experience during those years that, along with the inspired counsel of my friend (that Andrew was Heavenly Father's son first and mine second), finally *started* me on the path to understanding what true prayer is all about.

While living in Butte, Montana, my children attended Margaret Leary Elementary School. When my son Ryan was in the fourth grade, a young man in his class who had been taunted mercilessly by a bully brought a gun to school. In his effort to chase down and kill the bully, he killed a young boy who was an innocent bystander.

My son witnessed the killing and watched helplessly as his schoolmate began his exit from this world. The young killer, whose parents were both dying of AIDS, was without emotion even though he had killed an innocent victim.

I was in the middle of my daily walk at the mall when I received the news that a boy had been shot and killed at Margaret Leary Elementary. I was at the school within a matter of minutes. Yet those minutes seemed like the longest minutes of my life. During those agonizing minutes, I prayed like I had never prayed before.

With every fiber of my being, I wanted my son to be safe and not to be the one who had been shot. In that time of extremity, I wanted so badly to ask my Father in Heaven for my son to be spared. However, I realized that in doing so, I was asking for another parent to endure the grief I so passionately hoped to avoid. I couldn't do it; I knew in my heart it would be wrong. So, possessing a rare, submissive attitude, I pleaded that if my son had not been spared, I would somehow be strengthened to deal with his loss. I prayed for the ability to accept God's will, whatever it was.

Serving on the PTO board at Margaret Leary, I knew the school principal well. She was still on the playground where the shooting had taken place when I arrived. She let me know that my son had been spared. I was so grateful. Yet, even in my sublime gratitude, my heart broke for the family who lost their son.

I was a room mother that year for both my second grade daughter and my fourth grade son. After the shooting, as I helped in their classrooms, I could see that there had been more than one victim that day. The little second graders in my daughter's class, who had been on the back side of the building away from where the shooting had occurred, appeared as scared and traumatized as the many eyewitnesses in my son's class. It never occurred to me until I saw the faces of all the children that they might need prayers in their behalf as well.

That experience helped me understand what my position is in the heavenly scheme of things. It helped me to understand how wrong it was of me to ask for things that were not meant to be. It helped me to understand that I needed to allow Heavenly Father to be in charge and that I should be more willing to accept whatever I am called upon to deal with. The shooting at Margaret Leary began a makeover in my mind-set regarding prayer.

I believe there is a strong possibility that the boy who killed my son's schoolmate suffered from reactive attachment disorder (RAD). At that time, I would have never dreamt that such a disorder existed, let alone that I would be touched by it so personally.

Chapter Ten

THE TRAGEDY OF RAD

The life I envisioned for Andrew and Dina as we brought them home from Russia was full of sugar and spice and everything nice. My idealism energetically manifested itself with hopes of watching them live the American dream. Once language was no longer a barrier, I anticipated the thrill of watching them bring their talents and passions to life.

I was certain that coming from the background they did, they would have a greater sense and appreciation of the opportunities that living in a free and prosperous nation could afford them. I dreamed that, with a loving family supporting them, they would recognize and develop their God-given gifts without the apathy that sometimes accompanies those born with greater means and circumstances.

Our first year with the children was spent in helping them adjust, playing a constant game of charades until their comprehension of the English language was sufficient to communicate with words alone.

In Russia, as we met with our children for the second time, Dina came running to me crying "Mama, mama!" She clung to me in tears and did not want to let go of me. In our first seven years living together as mother and daughter, that was the one and only time that Dina clung to me or initiated any effort to ask me for assistance. At home, Dina most often kept herself removed from the rest of the family. Yet, with people other than immediate family, she was often charming and outgoing. Within a year of having her in our home, she began making accusations of mistreatment by her immediate family to extended family and people she barely knew. She seemed to like making people feel sorry for her. I was baffled by her behavior. It seemed that the very family members who made the greatest efforts to be supportive of her were the ones she targeted most with her negative accusations. Though several family members were the object of her contrived stories, I was made out to be the person who most wanted to make life miserable for her.

Andrew kept his distance emotionally as well, but he did not make accusations of mistreatment like his sister. Instead, he displayed other behaviors that did not make sense to me. Initially, he seemed to take becoming a member of our family in stride. He showed few if any signs that the adjustment was difficult. However, it eventually became apparent that he had difficulty in acknowledging and expressing emotions. Nothing seemed to excite him, at least that he was willing to admit. It was as though admitting wants, desires, and passions made him feel too vulnerable. Then, while living in St. Louis, he began stealing petty items from family and classmates.

Both children displayed a significant pattern of lying as their preferred means of communication and stubbornly refused to take any responsibility for their actions.

After raising four older children, I did not expect them to be perfect, nor did I expect a magical transformation with each of my efforts to teach them right and wrong. However, I did expect to see some sort of impact from my efforts. Instead, I seemed to affect them as much as an arrow thrown at a brick wall.

It was during our time in St. Louis that I discerned their abnormal behaviors more clearly. It was also in St. Louis that Dina became a teenager and everything seemed to escalate—her efforts to convince family and friends that we were abusive, her resentment against me, and her efforts to participate in self-destructive behaviors.

Their behaviors did not make sense to me. From my perspective, my two adopted children had gone from a Russian orphanage in a small village with a bleak economy and little chance of obtaining a fulfilling life to a family who loved them and a country filled with an abundance of positive opportunities. It wasn't exactly rags to riches, but it didn't make sense to me that they couldn't recognize the blessings they had been given.

I would remember some of our firsts with them: Dina running to me in the orphanage and not letting go, their first trip to Sam's Club and their amazement at the vastness of the store, their first trip to Walmart and their delight in the huge variety of items available for purchase, and their unreserved delight in jumping on our family trampoline for the first time. I couldn't understand why, when God had so clearly intervened in their behalf and blessed them with a life that presented them with so many favorable circumstances, their approach to life was filled with so much apathy and anger.

Particularly in Dina's case, it seemed as though a bitter message was trying to be communicated through behavior. The message seemed to say, "I'll teach you for loving me and trying to help me."

Andrew and Dina had been removed from their birth parents by the Russian government for neglect and abandonment. Yet, Dina idolized her birth mother and often insisted that we had wrongly removed her from Russia and the mother who "truly" loved her.

None of our efforts to help them seemed to succeed. One night, out of frustration, I decided to go online to try to find an adoption support group. My quest to find an adoption chat room was unsuccessful. So, feeling disgruntled and annoyed, I did another search. Pounding my fingers on the keyboard, I filled the Google search box with the following words: children who do not have a conscience. My Google search sent me to a link that described an emotional disorder called reactive attachment disorder (RAD). I had never heard of RAD. I clicked on the link and started learning about it.

As a result of finding the link about RAD, I found several informational websites dealing with RAD. The majority of the children with RAD had been adopted or been in foster care. I found that the disorder develops when the essential developmental bonding that normally occurs between child and mother does not take place. During those key months between the ages of six and eighteen months when we normally see infants exhibit a strong preference for their mother, RAD infants do not receive the care and safeguarding from their mothers that they need. As a result, crucial brain development lags or does not occur. In the case of my adopted children, they had been repeatedly left to fend for themselves as infants and young children. Their alcoholic birth parents had often left them locked and alone in their apartment while they partied. The information that I found explained that children with RAD are tremendously afraid of being emotionally vulnerable and, as a result, are control freaks that often use various forms of chaos and discord as their bizarre means of control.

Because God guided me to recognize each of my children's emotionally unhealthy behaviors prior to knowing about RAD, I was easily able to recognize them in the list of symptoms.

Some of those symptoms included: lying with no apparent reason, an attitude of entitlement and self-importance, triangulation of adults, false allegations of abuse, a severe need to control everything and everyone, trouble understanding cause and effect, stealing, and so on, and these worsen as the child gets older. Few of the symptoms I saw listed did not apply to my children.

Children with RAD tend to see their primary caretaker (who is usually the adoptive or foster mother) as their greatest threat. For a child struggling with RAD, nobody is to be trusted. However, the mother figure in their life is usually the person they work hardest to ostracize and hurt. For most RAD children, it is the birth mother's neglect and lack of safekeeping that has precipitated the emotional issues. Therefore, as a reaction to the pain and anguish caused by the birth mother, the children target the birth mother's replacement.

Finding the information on RAD made me feel as though I had been given an invaluable gift. For so long I had not been able to understand why my children behaved as they did (especially toward me), but after finding the information on RAD, so many of my questions were answered. I immediately ordered a book on raising children with RAD. It was called *When Love Is Not Enough* by Nancy L. Thomas. As a mother who had been traumatized by the behaviors of children with RAD, I felt the book offered me some rays of hope.

I was particularly hopeful where Dina was concerned. At the time, her behaviors were of greatest concern and she seemed to have the greatest need for help.

Once I learned about RAD, I pursued traditional therapy for Dina. Within a few short sessions with a therapist, who assured me that she was familiar with reactive attachment disorder, Dina had the therapist convinced that I was the epitome of the devil himself.

After our first fiasco with therapy, I learned that the best course of treatment for RAD children is therapy in which at least one parent is involved in the therapy sessions along with the child and a specially trained RAD therapist. This is because children with RAD tend to be extremely manipulative and generally have no issue with lying. I also learned that there were a few hitches in our situation with Dina: teenagers generally were more difficult to achieve success with, and it was important for parents to remain emotionally calm and neutral. That was a problem since I had already been pushed to my emotional limits. The daily stress of dealing with children, severe depression, and 24-7 migraine headaches had taken its toll. Chiropractic school made it impossible for my husband to be a dependable participant. I would need to be the principal parent involved. To have any chance of effectiveness, I needed to be in a place emotionally where I could nurture Dina and not let her get to me.

I wasn't sure what to do; this dilemma was of such enormity that I felt that prayers alone would not be sufficient. I set aside a day to both fast and pray. I asked for answers and for the strength to be able to follow through with whatever answer I was given.

A few days later, our grown kids started showing up to spend the Christmas holidays with us. In the confusion and hubbub of everyone being together, I wasn't expecting a quick answer. I thought I might receive God's reply after everyone went back home. However, somehow it happened that for a brief moment, I was alone in a place that was quiet. In that short moment, a voice spoke to me and said, "She needs residential treatment." As it always does when I receive personal inspiration, I felt warm, powerful reassurances within my heart.

As soon as the holidays were over, I immediately started efforts to get Dina the treatment she needed and we wanted her to have. Not surprisingly, my efforts to get her treatment increased her hostility toward me. We eventually got her approved for treatment at Boys and Girls Town in St. James, Missouri. Her treatment there seemed to help her gain a better grasp of her emotional issues.

Eventually, Dina admitted that she targeted her anger and

resentment toward me even though she could see it belonged elsewhere. It takes a lot of work and desire for anyone to overcome emotional trauma. One of the biggest detriments for children with RAD in overcoming their emotional issues is their mind-set that they don't need anyone and that they can take care of themselves. I have found that God is always a key component in genuine healing. Rather than leaning on God and those who loved her, Dina chose to believe that she could handle her issues on her own. As a result, within about two weeks of her return back to our home, her anger and resentment began to manifest itself once again. Since that time, her emotional struggles have been a roller coaster ride of ups and downs.

Even though the treatment has not provided the long-term effects I would have hoped for, I believe with all of my heart that the therapy Dina received has enabled her to deal with her life on a more successful level than she would have been capable of otherwise.

I have tried to teach Andrew and Dina that although they are not to blame for their emotional issues, they must still be responsible for overcoming them. I have often used the example of breaking a leg in an accident caused by someone else's negligence; the injury was not their fault, but they still need to seek treatment for proper healing, and the appropriate exercises and therapy need to be utilized for the desired recovery to occur.

In the years since we adopted Andrew and Dina, I have enjoyed a few conversations with Micki Elmer, the woman who helped me find our children and whom I consider a dear friend, though contact is infrequent. During those conversations, we catch up with each other, and we always talk about how our children are doing. We also discuss the other families and children whose adoptions were facilitated by Micki's efforts. Though a voice did not speak to them, many other mothers (and a few fathers) were also guided to their children through inspiration.

We both find it tragic that most if not all of the Russian children have had significant emotional and behavioral issues and that their adoptive families have endured great heartache and rejection. It has made many of us, as adoptive parents, question why the inspiration was given to find our children and what purpose adopting the children has served, when they have rejected our efforts to help them.

Currently, I do not have those answers, but I do know that, in my family's case, our children were meant to be a part of our family. I may not have been told to find Dina, but I know that Andrew and Dina were meant to be kept together. I am completely confident that God knew we would want to keep them together and that it was unnecessary for Him to direct us to adopt Dina. I know that Heavenly Father's methods are not always easily understood by us as His children, but that doesn't make them any less perfect.

I know that those of us who have welcomed children into our families through adoption or foster care because of inspiration we received were not guided by a God who was intent on punishing us or making us suffer. The paths we have walked because those children have been a part of our lives *have* been filled with thorns, but they have also been jam-packed with learning experiences.

Each time I think about the difficulties we have experienced as we have raised our adopted children, I cannot help but also think about the classrooms I observed in premortality. As I think of those classrooms, I am reminded again and again that we came to this earth to learn. I am also reminded that it is not through our pleasant experiences that we are most effectively taught to be like our Father in Heaven. It is through our painful ones.

If there is one lesson I have walked away with after having lived with children with RAD, it is that we must make sure that the infants and toddlers of our world receive the love and nurturing they need. Our children are priceless, and we must not take our responsibility for them lightly. I am grateful that God has enabled me to understand the importance of loving and nurturing children. The stark contrast between the ability of my biological children and my adopted children to love and engage in healthy relationships has not been lost on me. I have witnessed that the ability (or lack thereof) to love in whole and healthy ways reaches out into all aspects of our lives.

Our willingness to love does make us vulnerable. When we choose to live a life filled with love, we can be certain that we will also experience loss and heartache as a result. However, God has shown me, and I have seen firsthand, that there is nothing more tragic than a crippled heart that is unable or unwilling to truly love.

Chapter Eleven

FINDING MY WAY
BACK TO HEALTH

*D*epression is a heinous monster. It left me so hollow and so listless. So many fires in my life went out. I lost my zeal for so many of those things I had once been passionate about. The only things that I still cared about were my family and my Creator. Unfortunately, although I never let up on my prayers and my scripture study, I could no longer feel my Creator's presence with me like I once had. Instead, I had to rely on my memories of what it had felt like to feel Him close and to consistently feel His influence. Though I knew from previous experiences that I was not alone, I still felt very much alone.

I have always been one of those individuals who truly enjoys being alone. I don't need sound for company. I don't always need to have someone to talk to. I love being with friends and family, but I am fond of silence as well. Silence has always been a friend to me. During my quiet moments I have most successfully communed with my Creator and most often received personal revelations.

However, during the months that I struggled with severe depression, a particular type of silence became very difficult for me. It challenged my peace and sense of well-being. It was not a silence that is free of sounds; it was the silence of being unable to commune with God as I once had. That silence made me feel strangely uncomfortable. I have always leaned heavily on my Heavenly Father for a sense of who I am. With my sense of self and my ability to feel His continual presence with me severely diminished, I became uncertain of who I truly was. Depression and its ability to inhibit my spiritual receptors made me feel as though I was in the constant company of a stranger.

With my struggling sense of self, it was often difficult for me to be around noise and people. I no longer felt comfortable or secure with even my closest friends. I felt like a space traveler who had been removed from her home planet. As friends and loved ones looked into my eyes, I wondered if they could see the ill-tempered, dark, massive void that seemed to fill my soul. Peace and contentment were so evasive I wondered if I would ever experience them again. The only people whom I was consistently able to enjoy being around were my husband, my children, and their teen friends who for so long had made our home their daily place to hang out.

People would ask me how I could put up with so many teenagers hanging around my house all the time. What they didn't know was that it was my husband and all those teenagers (my own kids and their close friends) who kept me going. The only time my life seemed to take on any semblance of normalcy was when I was in their company. My husband and all my "kids" were the only bright spots in an otherwise shattered existence.

My depression and ill health had a huge negative impact on our businesses. It was sheer force of will just to get out of bed every day. It was all I could do to get to the office a couple of times a week and attempt to take care of critical needs. Even when I made it to the office, it was rare that I could manage to put in more than one to two hours. I was in charge of everything financial, a huge problem since everything financial was a major depressive trigger for me. Almost without fail, handling financial matters would send my depression spiraling in a negative direction. Between my physical health and my emotional health, there was no way I could keep up with everything. I was both flailing and failing.

Prior to my depression, I had always considered myself to be a good person. Conducting my life with honesty and integrity had always been a high priority. However, once my life completely unraveled, I no longer knew what to believe about myself. My priorities had not changed, but what I had become was frighteningly foreign to me. The original framework was still there, but everything else about my life seemed to be under major reconstruction.

I didn't have to be a genius to see the catastrophic impact that my physical and emotional health was having on our businesses and my family. Unfortunately, my depression and internal voices made it next to impossible for me to separate the negative effects of my health from negative self-judgment of my character.

My doubts about myself led me to seek time in the temple. If I was truly a despicable character, I prayed I would be guided in how to turn myself around. If I weren't as bad as some—including myself—would have had me believe, then I prayed to find a new confidence in myself.

In September of 2002, as I entered the dressing room of the LDS temple in Cardston, Alberta, Canada, I received a communication from heaven. A voice of light told me that my spirit had been severely traumatized and that a portion of the pain that I suffered from was the anger and trauma that my spirit had experienced trying to express itself. I was told that in a very real way my spirit was like the earth. Just as the earth cries to heaven for justice when innocent blood is shed, my spirit was expressing itself in a similar manner. A portion of my pain was my spirit giving voice to its suffering.

That message filled me with awe, hope, and wonderment for all of about one day, and then the relentless pain that was a part of each day overwhelmed me once again and my ability to feel hopeful about my future resumed its previous dismal levels. (Fortunately, although that message did not have an immediate long-lasting effect, it did help me substantially as my time came to fully recover.)

I know that after this and all my past spiritual experiences, I should have been more convinced that I, like all of God's children, was a wreck worth salvaging. However, with bill collectors making their daily cynical calls, finances looking bleaker and bleaker, severe incessant pain, and feeling that I had become an overwhelming burden to my husband and children, it was as easy as slicing a hot knife through butter to convince my mind that I deserved to be trashed. It didn't help, of course, that my subliminal voice added its chant that I didn't deserve to live and should have never been born.

In an effort to find a more positive foothold, I sometimes tried to reach out to friends and loved ones with the hope that extending my circle of positive support would help my efforts to get better. However, my ability to communicate effectively was severely impaired by headaches and depression, so, as a result, very few of my friends and loved ones even realized my calls or visits were an effort to increase my support network.

Working to overcome my depression felt like climbing Mount Everest with only the tips of my fingers. Though a figurative description, that is literally how it felt. At the conclusion of so many of those days that I fought through depression, I marveled that I had any "fingertips" left to hold on with.

Many days, in order to survive, I would have to live minute by minute and sometimes even second by second. Expanding my horizon or making progress could not even be contemplated. I could only keep breathing and keep moving and hope that eventually the moments ahead would become easier.

Sometimes, at key moments, a word of encouragement would keep me determined to hang on; my husband was particularly adept at saying the right thing at just the right time. Unfortunately, at other times, remarks or events would crush me like a massive boulder and then, despite what anyone said, I could feel myself sliding into a deep, impenetrable chasm.

The roller coaster ride between making progress and losing my footing was incredibly frustrating. It became so hard to fight for progress when I knew in one fell swoop I could lose my footing and go sliding right back to where I had come from.

It was after experiencing a particularly deep and drastic slide that I decided to call it quits once and for all. The events of that particular day completely convinced me that I was an albatross to my family. I was certain my family would be better off without me. The uphill battle and painful slides had overwhelmed me. All my personal experiences with inspiration and heavenly guidance seemed irrelevant. It was that night, with all the fight gone out of me, that I got on my knees and said my good-byes to God, ready to take whatever consequences came from the actions I planned to take the next day. Thankfully, it was also that night that my beloved grandfather and loving Heavenly Father came to my rescue, allowing me to revisit my premortal life and my prebirth meeting with my Creator.

I am so grateful for the rescue efforts of my deceased grandfather and my Creator. Upon my return to my body, my battles were not eliminated and my depression did not vanish. However, though my life continued to be extremely challenging, my ability to reflect upon my meeting with my Heavenly Father enabled me to hang on with some additional calluses on my fingertips.

I wanted to experience the true intelligence and love of that realm again. I knew that to lose my battle with depression meant that I would never be part of that celestial sphere again. My life was not easier, but my resolve and understanding were greatly increased.

After my return to my body, although I could no longer remember all of the details of my life as I had viewed them in premortality, I was even more convinced that my physical health was an important key in improving my emotional health. I felt sure that attention needed to be directed toward previous accidents, illnesses, and health history. I knew that my health had not deteriorated overnight. I felt strongly that at least some of the causes of my current ill health were tied to prior health events. And from that point forward, I *knew* in a way that I cannot explain that I was meant to get better.

Sometimes we must be taken to a different place or mind-set in order to find healing. I had to be taken to both. God knew that I needed to be taken to a place where I could open my mind to a new paradigm and allow myself to physically rest. St. Louis became that place for me.

While living in Great Falls, Montana, I had allowed myself to run on adrenaline for too many years. Greg and I were managing two businesses and a family of six children, and I was in denial about the severity of my health issues.

Though my depression emerged while I was living in Great Falls, depression itself was only an aftereffect—my body crying for help and manifesting that there was something very wrong going on. And so were my 24-7 migraines.

I have since learned the importance of being still and deliberately setting aside time to ponder and meditate, but at that time in my life, it was unfathomable. The next deadline, responsibility, or commitment was always approaching.

My headaches were the first attempt by my body to let me know that something was wrong and needed to change, but I did not recognize it as such, so eventually my body tried to utilize the depression as well.

At that time, I believed the most important responsibilities I had to attend to were my family and our businesses. God was about to teach me that the most important business that I needed to attend to was me—not in a narcissistic or self-centered way, but in a healthy, whole, and self-loving way.

By late December 2002, I had exhausted efforts to find medical remedies for my headaches and depression. After bankrupting all the possible prescription remedies for my headaches and depression to no avail, I had been told by doctors that I needed to seek therapy because my problems were in my head. They seemed to think that if all available medications failed, then the only other possible solution had to be that I suffered from some variety of mental illness that induced me to seek unneeded medical attention and waste thousands of dollars of personal income that otherwise could have been put to better use.

I knew otherwise. I had already pursued therapy to help with any emotional issues that were impacting my life. I knew my body, I knew myself, and I knew that therapy was not going to bring an end to my headaches and depression. Therefore, I began to search for answers on my own.

Experience had taught me that persistence combined with heavenly help is always a winning formula. My Heavenly Father had already shown me numerous times that He was a ready and willing ally. The difficult part, for me, was that I knew that my alliance with God didn't necessarily mean that I would get answers when or where or in the form I desired—it would be His game plan, not mine. The wonderful part was that I knew that God had never let me down. My mortal experiences combined with my experience of revisiting my prebirth life absolutely convinced me that because of His perfect love and His complete, all-encompassing perfection, He never would let me down, nor could He. The only one in the partnership with my Creator that could fail or let me down was me.

Even though I knew that Heavenly Father would not and could not fail me, knowing my own weaknesses often caused me to have doubts. It was easy to try to second guess myself with questions like, What if I wasn't meant to get well? What if I had misunderstood something and was meant to be sick for the rest of my life and then be well in the next stage of my existence? What if there weren't any more answers or solutions to my health and it was my outlook or ability to deal with my life that was going to get well? I wondered if "well" could be defined as having an increased understanding of the purposes of this life. If that were the case, I would need to consider myself well without having made any progress in my physical or emotional health.

I found it a little disturbing and frightening when I had thoughts like that. However, something inside of me let me know that I couldn't give up.

After my experience in premortality and the twelve or thirteen years of headaches and other health maladies, I started learning to listen. I began to listen to my body, to my spirit, and, in a much more earnest way, to God. I believe that teaching me to listen was one of the most important things that God has ever done for me. I have always been blessed to be a very spiritual person, but when I started listening, a slow but steady transformation began to take place. Through listening, I was finally able to discern and eliminate those subliminal voices that had impacted me negatively for most if not all of my life. It was through listening that I came to understand, identify, and discern the voices of truth and the voices of deception.

It was through listening that my husband and I were guided to St. Louis—a new place where we learned a new mind-set.

Early in January 2003, I received inspiration that I needed to see a chiropractor I could trust. Greg and I traveled three and a half hours to see a chiropractor who was the son of a good friend. By following that inspiration, I hoped I would be blessed with a healing experience or some sort of remedy that would enable me to eliminate my headaches.

I walked out of the chiropractor's office feeling disappointed, but Greg walked out of the office awed by the experience he had just had. As we got into our car, he said, "You are never going to believe what just went on in there." Knowing of nothing spectacular that had happened while we were in the office, I asked, "What went on in there?" He said, "I am supposed to do this." Not knowing what he was referring to, I asked, "You are supposed to do what?" "I am supposed to become a chiropractor."

It took a few moments for me to overcome the shock of what he had just told me, but as soon as I did, confirmation of the inspiration that my husband had just received filled my heart. And it was a good thing that those feelings of warmth filled my heart so powerfully because as we drove home to Great Falls, the logistics of what it was going to take for my husband to become a chiropractor began to settle in.

As we sat down with our children to tell them about the dramatic change that was coming into all of our lives, my heart was breaking. I knew that I had to brace myself for the fact that I would probably be leaving some of them behind. Three of our children were legal adults and would need to decide if they were staying or coming with us.

Within five months, we had decided that we were to go to Logan College in St. Louis, Missouri. Greg was accepted into school, our children had been apprised of the new move that we were about to make, our home had been put on the market, and a fixer-upper in St. Louis had been purchased and made livable. Greg had started school, with the rest of us, less our two oldest children, joining him by the end of May.

In order for all of that to happen, I had to receive the inspiration to see a chiropractor I could trust, and Greg and I had to be removed to a place and situation that allowed us to receive the next, more important piece of inspiration that Greg was to become a chiropractor.

I could not have imagined the dramatic life changes that would occur during those years in St. Louis. The inspiration that guided us to pull up roots and move halfway across the country was powerful and strong, and there was not a single day that I did not sense that we had been guided there for a higher purpose.

A few weeks before we moved from Great Falls, as I worked furiously to assemble a large portion of our household for storage and prepared to move, I was given some inspiration of comfort. It said, "Great things will happen there (in St. Louis)."

Prior to moving to St. Louis, I had never been inclined to seek alternative health care. I was not raised utilizing alternative medicine, and when alternative cancer treatments in Mexico failed to save my grandfather, I made the error of believing that all alternative treatments were just a hoax.

As I became assimilated into the mind-set of chiropractic care, I realized that the chiropractic point of view was where my belief system had always been aligned. For years, I had attempted to utilize the expertise of doctors (MDs) but most of those efforts had left me feeling frustrated. Once I understood that MDs look to match symptoms with medication, I understood why I had been so discouraged. My personal mind-set had always been to find the source of the problem and then figure out a way to remove the cause or, at the very least, alleviate the cause.

Guiding my husband back to school to become a chiropractor and relocating us to St. Louis seems to have been Heavenly Father's way of saying, "I have answers to your prayers, but first I need to move you to a place where you can heal and develop a different mind-set."

True to God's promise to me, great things did happen in St. Louis. It is truly amazing what happens when we let go of thinking that we are the only ones who can successfully navigate our path in life and allow God to guide us.

Prior to receiving the direction to become a chiropractor, Greg had been thinking about taking a few college courses, but nothing on the scale that the chiropractic college required. Greg was already a loving individual. God then enabled Greg to recognize his passion for helping people heal by sending him to chiropractic college. As an individual who has seen too many practitioners who seem to be oblivious to their patients and their needs, I believe it is truly a godsend whenever and wherever a doctor can be found who practices his craft with love and integrity.

I arrived in St. Louis with 24-7 migraines, severe depression, exhausted adrenal glands, and a digestive system that was in disrepair. (I was only aware of the first two issues.) Within a few months, the doctors in the student center at Logan Chiropractic College had taken me under their wings in an effort to help me find answers and to help me get well.

As my husband worked hard at his studies, I worked hard at getting well. Answers did not come quickly, but they did come. Once the doctors did blood work, they determined that I had issues with my adrenal glands and digestive tract. Those issues were addressed with supplements and keeping my nervous system regularly tuned. Over time, we unearthed the cause of my headaches. Monosodium glutamate (MSG) was the culprit. As I eliminated MSG from my diet, my headaches dropped in half. Once I was educated to the fact that MSG hides under other names, my headaches were virtually eliminated. As my headaches subsided and my body healed, my depression made its exit as well.

I am condensing in a few paragraphs a period of about four years. The healing that had occurred by the end of those years did not happen overnight. However, my health had not deteriorated overnight either. I suffered through migraine headaches for approximately fifteen years, and I undoubtedly started reacting to MSG at some point prior to my headaches materializing.

I experienced many ups and downs as I worked with the doctors at Logan. Yet as I relied upon my Supreme Creator to guide me, I was strengthened through the difficult times and was led to every answer I needed as I was prepared to receive it.

After being sick for so long, I forgot what it was like to be well. As I made progress in my recovery, Heavenly Father helped me understand that I needed a healthier paradigm to operate from as well. Within just a few days, I came across two books that reminded me of the power of my mind-set: *Stone Soup for the World* and *As a Man Thinketh* by James Allen. Finding those books was not a coincidence, and I knew that as I read them. There is always a "knowing" that occurs when I am led to someone or something by God. I always know that my encounter with that person or that information is not coincidence but is for my benefit. As I read those books, they helped me to realize that I needed to once again think like a well person.

After fifteen years of being sick, it was hard to remember what my thoughts had been like when I was well. Yet as I did, I began to recall some of the passions I had enjoyed when I was well: drawing (observing shapes, shadows, and ratios and making things come to life on paper), being outside and enjoying the sunshine on my face, reading a good book, and organizing gatherings with friends.

My headaches and depression had severely hindered my ability to participate in and enjoy those activities that had once been some of my passions.

In guiding me to those memories of my passions and helping me to create a new and improved state of mind, God also provided a reminder of how important it is to give place to those passions. I'm not talking about sexual passion here; I'm talking about those God-given talents and abilities that we have been blessed with and that we have a love and enthusiasm for. Those passions provided me with great joy, and I needed to make them a consistent part of my life.

I realize that many may ask why they or their loved ones have not been granted healing or some other miracle that they have sought in their lives. I do not have those answers. What I do know is this: prior to this life, we were each an active participant in planning and deciding the kinds of trials and learning experiences we would have here on earth. The severity of the trial or difficulty was not our biggest concern. Our biggest concern was the ability of each trial to help us become like our Heavenly Father, and we were never forced or coerced into any decision. It never has been and never will be the character of our Creator to force us or remove our ability to choose.

Many times I have looked to heaven and asked why. If I could still remember all of the elements of the mission I agreed to before my mortal birth, I am sure my reactions to many experiences would have been changed or at the very least tempered. I'm now inclined to skip asking why and to simply ask how—how am I to do this or how would you like me to handle this?

I have seen and been granted many miracles in my life, but I think I can safely say that in each instance, I was expected to listen for the answers that I prayed for and then provide the appropriate response when I received it.

All of those years that I was sick with migraines, I worked diligently to find answers. I knew in my heart that I was expected to do my part. I can absolutely attest to the fact that when the guidance came to my husband that he was to become a chiropractor, I knew that in some way that guidance was an answer to my prayers. For reasons we didn't understand at the time, we needed to be removed to a different place and to embrace a different mind-set.

Had we not been willing to listen and then act, I would not have experienced the miracles that I have. My miracles did not occur without sacrifice. But after moving halfway across the country and my husband enduring a very rigorous curriculum, the difficulties seem to pale in contrast to what we have gained. The point that needs to be emphasized here is that when we are willing to ask for God's help and then to listen and respond to His guidance, we are never disappointed. Answers come and miracles happen.

Most of my answers and miracles have occurred during those times when I have been the most proactive and optimistic. I do not believe that this is a coincidence. As Thomas Dewar said, "Minds are like parachutes—they only work when open."[1] It is undeniable that many of my health miracles have come as a result of my being open to new information and fresh perspectives. I believe that when we open our minds and hearts and are willing to add our physical and mental efforts as well, we open doors wide open for God to help us. It is when we do this that I believe we become more likely candidates for the literal miracles.

I never thought I would live to see the day I would actually express gratitude for going through severe depression. Yet, today, I am extremely grateful for that experience. I now understand that my depression created the need for many questions to be answered, much soul searching and self-evaluation to be done, and a restructuring of my life that would not have happened otherwise. I feel extremely fortunate that the rebuilding process was done with my Father in Heaven's consistent guidance. My Father's assistance has guided me through many difficult moments, taught me to truly listen, and helped me find and see many important truths, and it has provided me with a new yet superior foundation from which to operate my life. My new foundation is the springboard for improvements in every aspect of my life. As a result, I am now able to live a life guided by love rather than fear, to honor my needs and myself, and to still have plenty to give.

I am indebted to my Heavenly Father for his willingness to work with me and guide me to a place of healing. It does not matter from what source or how the healing has been accomplished; I have seen

His hand in it all. I know He could have accomplished the same job with one incredible miracle, but then we both would have missed out on all the lessons I have learned. I, for one, feel blessed that He chose for me the better way.

Note

1. "Thomas Dewar quotes," ThinkExist.com, accessed 1 May 2011, http://thinkexist.com/quotes/thomas_dewar/.

Chapter Twelve

VOICES OF TRUTH

I love that Heavenly Father's voice is always a voice of truth. What I do not always love is that it often takes so much effort and obedience on my part before I can hear what He has to say.

I have been given messages from my Father in Heaven in many different ways. I have received messages through my conscience and from the Holy Ghost. I often sense God's direction when I study my scriptures, and I have heard His voice through guided and inspired humans. I have had words spoken to me by unseen messengers, I have been spoken to by the voice of my Savior, and, when I was taken back to the premortal existence, I saw that I have literally conversed with God. No matter what the method of communication, I always feel the confirmation in my heart that I am hearing voices of truth.

While in each instance the method of delivery may be different, there are some definite consistencies in the messages I receive from my Creator and those who serve Him. Their messages never contain lies or misdirection, nor are they ever in opposition to eternal truth. I may not always be told what I want to hear, but I am always told what I need to hear.

Their voices are always quiet and respectful. They may imply urgency, but they never scream or yell. The impact of the messages I have received has varied. Sometimes when I have received impressions, it has been easy for me to write them off as just trivial thoughts instead of the true inspiration that they are. However, since this is the way I receive the majority of my inspiration, I keep working at paying better attention to those types of messages.

I often feel impressions or promptings in the form of a gentle nudge, kind of like a peaceful reminder. Frequently, in the short term, the impressions and promptings that I receive seem trivial or of no great importance (especially when I receive those impressions during really inopportune times). However, in the long term, every prompting or impression that I have heeded has resulted in some needed benefit (for me or someone else).

Unlike my gentle promptings, hearing voices from heaven has had a dramatic impact on me. Those experiences have not seemed like a gentle nudge at all. When a heavenly voice told me that my daughter Dina needed residential therapy, I was left feeling no doubt whatsoever that was what she needed. I didn't understand why it was needed or why a less dramatic form of treatment would not suffice, but I knew the source of the guidance, and I knew that God knew better than I did. (And, of course, my heart confirmed the truth of everything that the voice told me.)

The voice of my Savior has had the greatest impact. I heard an audible voice when I was instructed that Dina needed residential treatment and both times I was told to find Andrew. Yet, although the message that Dina needed residential treatment had a powerful effect on me, it did not leave me shaking, weak, and struggling to be coherent of my surroundings like the messages to find Andrew did. Afterward, I was inspired to know that it was the voice of my Savior that spoke to me.

Those messages from my Savior left a unique, indelible imprint. I was left feeling as if I had somehow been lifted and filled with light and love. Yet at the same time I was left feeling drained and shaky—almost as though a strong electrical current had coursed through my body.

There is a consistent pattern that my Creator utilizes to guide me: As I am prepared, I am led to ponder on things. As I ponder on things, questions arise. As questions arise, I ask for answers. According to my efforts and preparation, I am then given answers.

I believe that growth pattern is inspired by God. It is all a learning process—a step-by-step evolution gauged exactly to my level of diligence and understanding, just like I witnessed with each of us in heaven. I love that our understanding builds as we allow it.

It was through that pattern that I was inspired with the knowledge of who had spoken to me when I was told to find Andrew. Several scriptural verses referring to communications with Deity seemed to describe similar feelings that I'd had. After reading those verses, it seemed only natural to ask if it had been my Savior who had spoken to me. My answer was that it was.

After I received that answer, my understanding continued to grow. Reading my scriptures became even more meaningful to me because I was able to internalize more deeply that what I was reading were the experiences of people who were just as human as I was. It also gave me more hope because I realized that we each have amazing potential when we allow ourselves to be guided by God.

As I seek to know and understand truth, the cycle continues: I gain some aspect of knowledge, knowledge leads to more questions, I seek and pray for guidance, I receive more answers (knowledge), I have more questions . . . and so it continues.

Although they may come with varying degrees of intensity, without fail, all communications I have received from Heavenly Father and those who assist Him have been accompanied by feelings of reassurance and warmth in my heart. Their messages never try to threaten or control. I may be commanded to accomplish a task, but it is always done in a way that allows for my refusal. Their messages are personal. I am only given instruction for myself and those I have responsibility over. I am never given direction for those who are outside of my natural sphere of authority.

I used to think that the voice of my thoughts was the voice of my brain, but when my spirit was removed from my body and taken back to witness the meeting with God in my pre-earth life, my thoughts stayed with my spirit. That experience taught me that the voice of my thoughts is the voice of my spirit.

In that sphere where God resides, truth and love reign supreme. In heaven, any thoughts filled with fear, hate, and false logic disappeared. Though my basic character and personality remained the same, the difference in the purity of logic and the depth of understanding was incredible.

The immense contrast between the voice of my thoughts in my mortal existence and the voice of my thoughts in heaven did not escape me. I now find myself craving that "perspective of truth" that I experienced in my premortal state. The purity of understanding and logic there was absolutely glorious and wonderful.

In the time since then, I have spent many hours contemplating that experience and the vast differences between the two spheres of existence. It may seem deceptively simple, but the main difference between heaven and earth is the level of truth and love that permeates each sphere. Were we to fill the earth with love and truth, we literally would have heaven on earth.

Our ability to love in whole and healthy ways is reliant on our understanding of truth and our willingness to implement those truths into our lives.

It was once a challenge to truly love and value myself. Early on in my depression, I realized that an internal voice of deception spoke to me on a daily basis. That voice of deception convinced me that if I ever allowed myself to rest—if I ever quit wearing myself out trying to make life wonderful for my family—they would quit loving me. I didn't feel that I had to give my children anything and everything they wanted, but I did have a real hang-up about my ability to be the wife and mother that my family deserved.

I thought recognizing that voice of deception would be a leap in my progress. Instead, it was only a step. Not realizing that Heavenly Father generally gives answers in a piece by piece fashion rather than all at once, I thought that, once I had been given the inspiration to recognize my voice of deception, all I would need to do was implement some changes, and my depression would be gone.

After continuing to struggle through severe depression for three or four more years, I became extremely frustrated that it was taking so long to get through the sinkholes and valleys and find some real vistas. It seemed as though the whole process was being unreasonably drawn out. I then had an experience that allowed me to see that I had not fully grasped everything my quiet voice of deceit communicated to me. This is my journal entry for that day:

Today was a breakthrough day. Though to everyone around me the transformation that has taken place inside of me may be barely perceivable, the change I know I have experienced will have a profound influence. For months and months and years, I have worked to determine what I was all about. Many things I knew were true from a logical standpoint (I was loved, liked, and so on), but I couldn't seem to internalize that knowledge. That inability left me hanging, and I knew it impeded my progress. I have prayed for help in this regard for a very long time. I have received some help, but I knew I needed more. This morning an answer came. I wish I could describe how quietly the answer came. At the same time, I wish I could describe the profound effect the answer had on me. In the silence of the morning, with no sounds from anything but my own thoughts, I finally heard an inner voice. The voice told me that I should have never been born, that the world would have been better off without me. The voice said I was a horrible mistake. As soon as I recognized the voice—as surprised as I was to hear it—I realized that the voice had spoken to me all of my life. I had heard it for as long as I could remember and yet at the same time I had not recognized its continued presence.

Once I recognized all that my voice of deceit spoke to me, a transformation occurred, and it will continue for the rest of my life.

I often find that in order to communicate more effectively with me, Heavenly Father frequently guides me to a place or situation where His communications can more easily penetrate my thoughts, more forcefully communicate His message, or more efficiently get my attention.

Such was the case when Greg was instructed to become a chiropractor. For months, Greg had been feeling like he needed to go back to school. But what he'd had in mind was taking a few night courses to add to the large volume of business classes he had already taken.

Once received, it was plain to see that Greg's revelation was going to change life as we knew it. Our two oldest children had recently returned home from missions for our church, and I loved having my family back together again under the same roof. It was obvious that the chances of that remaining so were remote. There were no chiropractic schools in Montana, and the closest school was in Portland, over 700 miles away from Great Falls.

After researching and praying about schools, Greg and I decided that St. Louis, Missouri, was the place we were meant to go—even though St. Louis was 1500 miles away from our family home.

At that point, we sat down with our children to tell them about the dramatic change that was coming into our lives. Breaking the news tore at my heartstrings. We had three children over the age of eighteen; I knew that I had to brace myself for the fact that I would probably be leaving some of them behind. Each of them had to decide whether they would move with us or do something else. When decisions were tallied, our two oldest children chose to stay behind.

My most difficult job as a result of our move to St. Louis was saying good-bye to them. Preparing for our move was a lot of work, but to this mom, who is so deeply attached to her children, those efforts seemed trivial in comparison. Unfortunately, I can't show you snapshots as proof, but I know I was surrounded by heavenly help, because I could feel the strength of their voices. There's no way I could have voluntarily left a part of my family and moved 1500 miles away on my own strength and understanding alone—especially when it was clear we would be starting over again at a time in our lives when many are turning thoughts toward retirement. I am a strong person, but when it comes to my family, I am not generally cooperative in regard to lengthy voluntary absences. It was the strength of the voices from heaven that buoyed me and enabled me to move to St. Louis.

By the time we left St. Louis, none of our four oldest children remained in our home. Three of our children had married. Throughout our time in St. Louis, we were blessed with several occasions to reunite with our children. Being together was always wonderful—it was the good-byes that were always difficult. However, each time I had to say good-bye, the same experience was repeated over and over again: I would be overwhelmed with powerful assurances in my heart, and an understanding beyond my own was communicated to me from heaven. Those divine assurances warmed me each and every time, powerfully conveying to me that we were meant to be in St.

Louis, that our entire family would be blessed for our sacrifices, and that ultimately we would be okay. Those voices from heaven made all the difference. Because of the strength and power of those voices of truth, I never once questioned or doubted that we were meant to be in St. Louis.

What I now understand is that my life is like one continuous motion picture reel, with adventures both big and small constantly being spliced into the film. Each adventure is an essential part of the picture of my life, but more important, how I work through and handle each adventure both great and small will ultimately determine the success of the end product. My efforts to live a moral life will not eliminate all of the adversities. However, since I want the picture of my life to ultimately become a masterpiece, living an exemplary Christlike life still needs to be my goal. The purpose of my life is to learn, but more important, I need to strive to improve and to follow God's admonitions for me. Therefore, I now see every experience as an opportunity to improve myself, develop greater faith, increase in knowledge and wisdom, and, most important, become more like my Creator.

I know from my experience in premortality that our spirits naturally crave wisdom and intelligence. I also know how easily we can be fooled by the voices of deceit that exist in this world.

It is because of that innate desire to gain knowledge that most of us, even after very difficult experiences, would not eliminate those experiences from our lives. We instinctively know that we would have to give up the knowledge gained by those experiences as well.

I also understand that the difficulties we endure in our lives are not always punishments from God. In fact, if we are doing our best to live His commandments, they are never punishments. Nevertheless, He does allow us to go through difficult experiences that are not of our own making in order for us to learn lessons that we could not learn in any other way.

God's lessons for me the last few years seem to be aimed at opening my mind and enabling me to see a much bigger picture than I have ever seen before. The closeness of my relationship with Him undeniably enhances my ability to learn from those personalized lessons. The closer I am to Heavenly Father and the more I rely upon

His guidance, the easier my lessons are learned. Whenever I am resistant, rebellious, disobedient, or self-centered, my ability to learn and listen comes to a screeching halt.

The closer I draw to God, the easier it is to discern and learn from His voices of truth. In fact, all of the voices in my life become easier to discern. Voices of truth never look to control, harm, or threaten. Instead, they lift, teach truth, and strengthen in positive ways. They lighten my burdens, and they light my way. What they have to say always improves my relationship with my Creator, and they seek to teach, build, and improve me. Voices of deceit always look to distance me from my Creator. They initiate doubts, fears, and insecurities. As I have observed my life and the lives of others, I have also seen that voices of deceit seek for control in ways that are contrary to God's will. Voices of deceit may be quiet and subtle or they can be overbearing and loud. However, the volume or source of deceitful voices are not the most important criteria—what matters most is that I am able to discern and then eliminate them.

Chapter Thirteen

THE FATHER I HAVE
COME TO KNOW

How do you describe the meaning of words like *love, perfection, compassionate, intelligence, light, master,* and *celestial?* Are they not best understood from a perspective of feeling rather than documentation? How do you describe a being of love, perfection, compassion, intelligence, and light, who is master of the universe and celestial in nature, when the descriptive words themselves are neither adequate nor vast enough to encompass what needs to be understood by the receiver in an indelible way?

I believe the answer is both simple and complex: You utilize the best available words, and then you turn the rest of the process over to that very Being who you are trying to describe—with the knowledge that within each of us is a spiritual heart created by Him, whose purpose is to teach us, enable us to know right from wrong, and testify of Him as our Creator.

"Truth is what the voice within tells you," Mahatma Gandhi said.[1]

From time to time, I have heard people say things like "If there was a God, there wouldn't be any wars" or "If God loved me, He wouldn't let things like this happen" or "If God were real, there wouldn't be so many mean people in the world" or "What does God care? We're all the same to Him anyway."

I witnessed in the premortal life that each of us was treated as a unique individual. We were never compared to or expected to perform according to another's capacity or ability, we were only expected to perform according to our own particular abilities. Each of us was honored for our unique qualities and potential.

I believe that in order to understand our world and our potential, we must know and understand our Creator. The Father of our spirits is not just a genius. He is not just the most amazing "man" ever known; He is an absolutely perfect being without a single flaw. His ability to love and His comprehension are all-encompassing. He is a God of love, intelligence, and truth, who is aware of every minute detail concerning each and every one of His creations.

As I observed the classrooms in the premortal existence, it was made clear that mortality would present us with challenges, weaknesses, and evil. The ultimate concern taught to us was not that those things would be present in our mortal lives, but how we would respond to them.

Each of us was involved in choosing the types of mortal experiences we would have, and we knew that the God-given gift of free choice would continue with us as we came to earth. We clearly understood that those mortal tests and trials would present us with the best opportunities to grow and become more like our Father in Heaven.

As we observe evil and opposition in this world, we are not seeing a testament to God's imperfection or lack of caring. We are witnessing the absolute fact that our ability to make choices is an eternal truth. God's laws and this world are predicated on eternal truths. By divine mandate, we are free to create individually and collectively the world we want to live in.

Eternal truth is just that—eternal. It never goes away, and it never changes. For some who want to rationalize their choices and behaviors, this fact is probably less than comforting. But for those who seek true understanding, this fact is to be celebrated! That is why in His perfection, God directs us and governs this world according to eternal truth and His perfect knowledge, not according to our own understanding (or lack thereof).

God is unwavering in His sameness and His adherence to eternal truth. Put simply, this means that God's laws will never change. It also means that He will always continue to know us, love us, and succor us—and He will always do it perfectly.

By virtue of their eternal nature, the undying truths that I witnessed in premortality apply just as much in this world as they do in the one we came from. We were of infinite value and were loved unconditionally there, and we are of infinite value and are loved unconditionally here. In my Supreme Father's eyes, my value does not hinge on my pocketbook or possessions. I am loved without reservation regardless of my choices, failures, or successes. (Note that we are loved unconditionally; we are not blessed unconditionally.)

I think it is important to know that it was not considered arrogant or wrong to believe in myself and in my potential in that realm where God dwells. In fact, believing in my capacities, abilities, and talents was an important way of acknowledging the gifts my Divine Father had given me and recognizing His transcendent influence. What would have been wrong in that world (and is wrong in this one) is to believe that I could do anything of true value without the aid and assistance of my Maker. My ability to breathe, move, think, and be is totally dependent on our Supreme Creator. Yet, those gifts and more He freely and lovingly provides to each of us.

I know that what is most important in the Celestial realm where God dwells is what is most important here as well: love, truth, family, relationships, righteousness, and service. I know that our hearts will always tell us what is most important, but I also know that sometimes we allow what we feel in our hearts to be clouded by influences that are not from God.

I used to own a small inventory business. January was always a busy month for me. In those days before UPC codes and scanners, I did inventories using small handheld calculators with tapes. Once those inventories were completed in the stores, I would spend several hours at home calculating totals. I am fairly fast on a 10-key, so I kept my calculator humming as I inputted numbers for inventories. The droning sound of my calculator spitting out tapes would drown out the sounds around me for hours at a time.

One January afternoon as I sat glued to my calculator, I had the horrible feeling that something was wrong. I stopped working and listened. I could not hear anything unusual, so I went back to work. Again, a few minutes later, I felt something was wrong and I stopped to listen. Once again, I could not hear anything that seemed to call for my concern. I resumed my work again only to feel for a third time that I needed to listen for something that begged for my attention. As I listened the third time, I still could not hear anything, so I got up from my chair and started walking around my house. As I approached the door to my basement, I could hear a muffled voice. It was barely audible. I ran downstairs, and as I reached the bottom of the stairs, I realized that I was hearing a voice coming from our downstairs refrigerator.

My ever-curious son Chad had climbed into our downstairs refrigerator and shut the door, only to find himself locked inside. It was an old-style fridge that was used for extra perishables, and it had a latch on the door that allowed it to be opened only from the outside and not the inside. As I opened that fridge door and pulled my son out, I was so overwhelmed with gratitude that I had listened to those quiet promptings.

Yet, on other occasions, I have felt strongly prompted to take precautions or to safeguard items, and then I have rationalized away those feelings by convincing myself that I was just being too emotional or overzealous. Without expounding on the insignificant details, suffice it to say that in the long term, I have regretted not listening to those promptings.

The secret to being able to sense what I need to sense and to know if I am being divinely prompted is to regularly and consistently be quiet and take time to commune with my Creator. My Father in Heaven does not speak with the booming voice of Niagara Falls; He speaks to me with the peaceful voice of a gentle ocean wave.

In order to be in sync with my Father in Heaven, I need to deliberately set aside and utilize quiet opportunities to reflect and ponder on my life and allow myself to receive guidance from my Father in Heaven. For me, silence is not a void to be filled, it is an opportunity for instruction and peace. Virtually all studies and self-help information speak of our need to meditate and to experience moments of reflection and introspection. I have found that even when I do not deliberately seek God in my serene moments, I am still able to feel Him. Feeling the Patriarch of my soul is a source of great strength to me.

Each of us is blessed with what Mahatma Gandhi called the

"voice within." We may call it a conscience or we may call it our heart. There are lots of names for it: center, soul, spirit, inner voice, small voice, still small voice, and moral compass to name a few. The name doesn't matter nearly as much as the purpose.

It is through that voice within that I know right and wrong. It is also through that voice within that I most commonly receive promptings and receive confirmations of truth. I believe that voice within is a gift from God. Through it, He teaches me, warns me, comforts me, and testifies to me that He is real and that He loves me.

Many years ago, while I was camping in the mountains, I was awakened by an angel. The purpose of the angel's visit was to show me my center. My center was shown to me as a real part of my being—it was near my physical heart. I was taught that my center was the medium through which God could communicate with me. I was shown my center because it was surrounded by ugly, jagged, grayish-black rocks. Rays of light could escape from my center, but they were greatly impeded by the rocks. I believe the rocks I was shown were symbolic. Real or not, they represented difficult life experiences and the pain that I harbored from those incidents. I was instructed to remove all of those offensive rocks. I was taught that those rocks inhibited my ability to receive love, truth, and light from my Creator. Also, not surprisingly, they affected my ability to be emotionally and spiritually healthy.

As I have worked to make sure that my heart is uninhibited, I have received a truly profound understanding of how important our hearts are in our ability to live a genuinely full and satisfying life. As the "rocks" have been removed, they have been replaced with a greater propensity for gratitude and for cherishing my family and loved ones, and with a greater desire to live a purposeful and meaningful life.

I feel very fortunate to have been blessed with many spiritual manifestations and experiences. I testify with all of my heart that it does not matter whether you see God himself, hear His voice, see an angel, witness a miracle, or simply feel a quiet prompting in your heart—it is the manifestation in your heart that accompanies those events that is most important. We can forget what we see or hear, but we will never forget what we feel.

Our loving Father has placed us here on this earth to learn faith and to grow, but He has not left us empty-handed. The tools we need to accomplish our tasks are here with us.

Our hearts are a critical and essential part of our being. They are also an irreplaceable tool for guiding our lives. Our hearts communicate our Father's love for us. They teach us truth—those same eternal truths that reign and rule throughout all creation. Our hearts are a vital part of who we are, and we must listen to them and utilize them if we truly want to be happy, know who we are, and maximize our divine potential.

I have found that once I feel truth confirmed in my heart, I must work to internalize that truth. My heart needs to be open and receptive like a sponge, not covered in rocks and impenetrable like my heart was when the angel showed it to me. I know that it is not enough to know only in *theory* that God loves me. I must deeply know that truth within my heart.

Once I have some truth revealed to me, I must ponder on that truth and think about its application to me. I must work to internalize that each truth learned applies to me as much as it does to anyone else, and I must do my best to live my life in accordance with that truth.

Once, when my son Ryan was about three and a half years old, we were preparing as a family to go on vacation. As a part of those preparations, I was spending hours in my basement sewing room making summer outfits for my children. The day before we were to leave on vacation, my deadline was looming, and I was working frantically trying to get everything done.

Ryan came downstairs and wanted me to spend some time with him. I reluctantly shooed him off, telling him that I would spend lots of time with him when I was finished sewing the clothing for him and his siblings. I tried to pacify him with thoughts of how much fun we were going to have together on vacation.

Ryan left the room with a look on his face that broke my heart, but I rationalized that I would make it up to him later when I got my sewing finished.

About thirty minutes later, I went to check on Ryan. He was nowhere to be found. I looked everywhere I could think of inside our home, calling out his name as I searched. Next, I looked for Ryan in our neighborhood, screaming for him to come home. All of my efforts to find Ryan were unsuccessful.

We lived near an irrigation ditch, so I quickly enlisted the help of Greg, my children, and our neighbors. When our efforts turned up nothing, I called the police department. Some searched the streets and yards of our neighborhood while others walked the ditch banks.

I was slowly driving around my neighborhood, apprehensively looking for any sign of Ryan, when a couple of young neighborhood boys stopped me. One of the boys asked, "Lady, have you seen a little three-year-old boy dressed in footie pajamas?" Recognizing their description of my son, I tearfully answered, "No, but he is my son, and I am trying to find him too."

After searching inside our home and scouring our neighborhood for close to an hour and literally screaming his name everywhere we searched, my husband found Ryan asleep under a corner table in our downstairs family room.

Our small downstairs family room was crammed with several pieces of hand-me-down furniture. A chair and a couch butted up to both sides of the table that Ryan was found under. The table had a bottom shelf that stood only about four or five inches from the floor. Somehow, Ryan maneuvered himself under the table and fell fast asleep. Our screams had not roused him from his deep sleep, and the crowded furniture made him virtually impossible to see.

I think that sometimes our relationship with God can share some similarities with my experience of losing Ryan.

It was so easy for me to get wrapped up in the hubbub of my vacation preparations rather than take a little time with my young son; yet, as I discovered that he was missing, how quickly my perspective changed. In those anxious moments that I looked for my son, those new clothes meant absolutely nothing, but my three-year-old son meant everything.

When life has been busy, it has sometimes been all too easy to let other things vie for my attention and crowd out time for my Creator. Yet, when difficulties strike, I am quick to recognize how important He and the blessings I need from Him are.

In reality, Ryan was never lost at all—we just couldn't find him.

God is never lost either, but sometimes He is missing in our lives because He has not been included.

Though trials and tribulation are meant to be a part of our mortal experience, I know we were never meant to handle life alone. Our Maker is acutely aware of each of His children. He knows us, He knows our problems, and He knows how to best guide us through those problems. He is not a silent God, but He does not enter where He is not invited.

As I have gained a greater knowledge and understanding of our Father in Heaven and His divine attributes, my relationship with Him has been built with greater ease and my communication with Him has become more natural. The more I have come to know my Creator, the more I have felt drawn to Him and have known that I can trust in His assistance.

Though my trip to the premortal existence helped me to understand my Heavenly Father to a degree I never before fathomed, I am still awed and amazed by His crystal clear perspective and His unwavering patience with me. I often plod along like a blindfolded dimwit, and He helps me every inch of the way with a clear understanding of what it will take to maximize my efforts and my potential. Virtually all growth that is guided by my Creator requires me to stretch in some way that is uncomfortable. However, I never walk away from that process without being taught or reaping a reward that is invaluable.

All I have to do is initiate contact through prayer, listen for the answers He provides, and be obedient to the truth and guidance I am given. I emphasize "all" because although the process is simple, it is not easy and cannot be done without *sincere*, consistent effort.

I cannot overemphasize how important the power of prayer has been in the process of developing my relationship with my Father in Heaven. Through prayer and the answers I have received as a result of those prayers, I have been guided, strengthened, and enabled to accomplish tasks that I could have never accomplished otherwise. More important, throughout that process, I have been blessed to increase my knowledge and understanding of my Divine Mentor.

For years I dreaded the prospect of writing this book. Yet because God had told me that I *must* write this book, I knew that though

I did not understand the reasons why, it needed to be done. I am a deeply private person, and I knew I was going to have to share feelings, experiences, and inadequacies that I preferred to keep to myself. Because many of my experiences are of a spiritual nature, I knew that public knowledge of them would generally be met with a large degree of skepticism and disbelief. Although many of the events could be proven, others were just my word with no further substantiation.

If I had been given ten scoops of writing desire for every ten minutes that I agonized over the book, I would have written a bestseller in no time. However, that was not to be the case. Prayer was key in overcoming my resistance to writing a book. Eventually, in answer to my prayers for help to overcome my hesitance, I began to have experiences that gradually gave me a desire to share my experiences.

Several of my life experiences helped me to be much less judgmental and more inclined to love my fellow man. Having this greater love was an important step for me. It blessed me with a stronger desire to help my friends and neighbors and subsequently be willing to endure some really hard writing moments in order to do so.

As I focused less on myself, it seemed as though an ever-increasing number of friends and acquaintances began sharing their problems with me. Their difficulties seemed to beg for a greater understanding of Heavenly Father—an understanding that I had and they seemed to need. I would listen to their stories, knowing an increased ability on their part to better understand Heavenly Father and the purposes of life would shed a much different light on their problems and, as a result, lighten their load. Many of them were feeling overburdened and alone. I wanted to be able to share my experiences with them, but, in most cases, time and circumstances did not allow me to do so.

Overcoming some of my fears of writing this book has, at times, felt like I was scaling the Himalayas. Yet, when I turn around and get a real look at the terrain that I have traversed, I can see that it has merely been a consistent series of bumps in the road. Because my heart has been able to change, my perspective has changed as well, and I have been able to make mole hills out of mountains.

I don't know that I have ever spent so much time in any one effort and still felt like such a novice. The volume of tears shed while my fingers picked at the keyboard may have single-handedly kept the facial tissue industry in the black. Yet, the process has had a purifying effect, one that I would never have anticipated.

Throughout the writing process, not a single tear or twinge of anxiety has been experienced that has not been buoyed by strength and reassurance from heaven. I would like to think that this book can be an example of what can be accomplished with determined, continuous efforts directed by our Divine Guide even though time and talent are not abundant. More important, I hope this book communicates God's love and His personal interest in each of us. We may each have different life experiences, but I know with all of my being that my loving Father in Heaven is totally aware of and devoted to each of His children. More of us will live happily ever after when we learn to lean on His perfect understanding and trust in His desire and ability to help us instead of relying solely upon ourselves.

William Wordsworth wrote,

> Our birth is but a sleep and a forgetting;
> The Soul that rises with us, our Life's star,
> Hath had elsewhere its setting,
> And cometh from afar:
> Not in entire forgetfulness
> And not in utter nakedness,
> But trailing clouds of glory do we come
> From God, who is our home[2]

I believe that we come to earth "trailing clouds of glory"—with a literal piece of our Celestial Father embedded in our soul. As the literal spirit children of God, we carry His imprint. Even though our memories of our premortal lives are temporarily "out of order," sprinkles of stardust from that celestial sphere whence we originated still make themselves known. Our hearts tangibly know the intangible. In addition to what we feel in our hearts, abundant evidence of our Loving Father surrounds us.

True to His promise to me in the premortal world, He has never, ever, not even for a moment, left me—and I know He never will. Although He presides over us from a place that is galaxies from this earth, God's love, support, and sustenance is very much here with each of us.

The Father of Eternity always strives to transform His children into something better, nobler, and more praiseworthy, and He does so while succoring us and loving us regardless of the place we are at or the resistance we give Him.

When men try to change a man, they try to surround that man with something better. Mankind tries to change his fellow man from the outside in. God knows the true way to change a man. He changes a man's heart. He changes a man from the inside out. Then, with his heart changed, that man changes the world around him because, for him, the world has already changed.[3]

My supernal Father is the epitome of magnificence, divinity, and majesty. There are so many glorious words available in the languages of the world, yet each one of them is so limited in its ability to describe the whole and perfect Being that my all-knowing Father is. The most magnificent words stand humbled and inadequate in their ability to communicate the full glory of God.

The Eternal Father that I have come to know knows me better than I know myself. I may have some idea of the talents I possess and the potential that is mine to develop. However, my experiences have shown me that any vision or dream that I have for myself is deficient unless it is guided by the perfect understanding of my Supreme Creator. He is the one with the complete picture of me and my potential; He has the full comprehension of how I can be happiest, feel most fulfilled, and best accomplish my unrealized possibilities.

No mortal father has ever been nor will ever be as loving, temperate, or concerned about his children as the Father of my spirit is. No friend has been or ever will be a truer friend to me than my Celestial Associate. No anchor could give me shoring against the storms of life than what my Loving Bastion provides. No mentor could mentor me with the passion, intelligence, and devotion that is never-endingly available from my Heavenly Counselor.

Suffice it to say that the God I have come to know knows and loves me, and He knows and loves you. He loves each of us with the kind of love and perfect knowledge that can inspire and transform us. He is not a complacent God that looks to excuse or rationalize our sins and misdeeds. He is, however, a merciful God who desires to help us overcome our weaknesses, difficulties, and transgressions and become heirs to all blessings, truth, and joy that eternity has to offer.

There once was a time when I believed that evidence of God's love for me was to be found in the absence of difficulties and problems. I now know that the amount of adversity in my life has no bearing on how much my Heavenly Father loves me. I have come to this earth to build my faith and reach my potential. As I proceed with the task of becoming all that I am capable of being, I am unfailingly surrounded with abundant evidence of His love.

I have had a taste of heaven, where love and truth prevail. Life on earth provides me with opportunities to have "nibbles" of heaven each and every day. Those nibbles do not come by accident. They must be sought after. It is in love, truth, and our Supreme Creator that they are found. I am grateful for a loving Father who diligently guides me to recognize truth and then shows me how to implement it into my life so that I can live a life increasingly filled with slices of heaven.

Notes

1. Full Quote: "Truth is what the voice within tells you. Truth and nonviolence are perhaps the active forces you have in the world. Truth alone will endure; all the rest will be swept away before the tide of time." Mahatma Gandhi, Gandhi International Institute for Peace, http://www .gandhianpeace.com/quotes.html.
2. William Wordsworth, *The Complete Poetical Works* (London: Macmillan and Co., 1888).
3. Ezra Taft Benson said essentially the same thing but in a little different way: "The Lord works from the inside out. The world works from the outside in. The world would take people out of the slums. Christ takes the slums out of the people and then they take themselves out of the slums. The world would mold men by changing their environment. Christ changes men, who then change their environment. The world would shape human behavior, but Christ can change human nature" (Ezra Taft Benson, "Born of God," *Ensign*, Nov. 1985, 6). Either way it is explained, the divine truth is that change comes from within.

CONCLUSION

*M*y heart reverberates with the love that my Eternal Father has for me. He is truly a Master of all light, truth, and knowledge. I am grateful for His perfection. I am thankful to know that He is always aware of me and that He is always willing to succor and mentor me. I am grateful to know that as I am called upon to experience trials and difficulties, I can unfailingly lean upon His crystal clear perspective, with a sure knowledge that I will be given the guidance and direction I need, whether or not it is the guidance and direction I want. I feel blessed to know that it is His ultimate intention to help me build a life based on eternal truth so that I may be granted rich, eternal blessings. I am grateful to know that helping me (and all of His children) to love, serve, gain intelligence, and cultivate potential is among His greatest desires and an all-important part of His plan for me. Also, I am deeply grateful to know that my loving Eternal Father honors my individuality. As I work to become all that I am capable of becoming, He will guide me step by step to a place of unique potential that is mine alone to obtain and that will provide me with the most earthly happiness and eternal joy.

It is my prayer that each of us, as a child of our Divine Father, will come to know Him as we all knew Him before this earth life. That, as we take our last mortal breath, our passionate and ever-loving Advocate will embrace us once again, and as He welcomes us home, amid His heartfelt expressions of love, He will commend us for living a life filled with love, purpose, and truth. That, as we join that next sphere of existence, great eternal blessings will be ours to enjoy.

ABOUT THE AUTHOR

*J*oAnna Oblander is happily married to her husband of over thirty years, Dr. Greg Oblander. She is the mother of six children, two of whom were adopted from Russia. Though her two most important jobs have been wife and mother, she has also been involved in a variety of businesses, church leadership responsibilities, and youth organizations, and she has been the lead organizer of a large biennial women's event. As a benefactor of many varied life and spiritual experiences, she has gained a strong conviction of the importance of knowing God and His true character. The knowledge and insights she has gained as a result of her experiences have taught her of the importance of gratefully recognizing, acknowledging, and developing our God-given capacities. Those experiences have instilled in her a strong desire to create an eternally meaningful life guided by God and has led her to seek a life that is in harmony emotionally, physically, and spiritually. Her greatest joys are being with her husband, children, and grandchildren and bringing health to others as she works with her husband in his chiropractic office.